921
GAN

Torgersen, Don
Arthur, 1934-.

Gandhi

DATE			

© THE BAKER & TAYLOR CO.

People of Destiny

A Humanities Series

There comes a time,
we know not when,
that marks
the destiny of men.

Joseph Addison Alexander

People of Destiny

GANDHI

By Don Arthur Torgersen

 **CHILDRENS PRESS, CHICAGO**

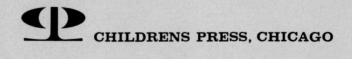

*The editors wish to express
their appreciation to Mr. Meyer Goldberg,
who created the series and inspired
the publication of* People of Destiny.

Cover and body design: John Hollis

———————

Project editor: Joan Downing

———————

Assistant editor: Elizabeth Rhein

———————

*Illustrations: Harley Shelton, Ron Kangles
—Hollis Associates*

———————

Research editor: Robert Hendrickson

———————

*Photographs: From the files of Wide World
Photos, Inc., Information Service of India,
Historical Pictures Service, Brown Brothers,
and Radio Times Hulton Picture Library.*

———————

Typesetting: American Typesetting Co.

———————

Printing: Regensteiner Press

*Quotations on pages 16, 46, 48, 50, 53, 58-59, 69, 76, 82, and 84
from* The Life of Mahatma Gandhi, *by Louis Fischer. Copyright,
1950 by Louis Fischer. Reprinted by permission of Harper &
Row, Publishers, Inc., and Jonathan Cape, Ltd. Quotations on
pages 38-39 and 53 from* Gandhi: His Life and Message to the
World, *by Louis Fischer. Copyright 1954 by Louis Fischer.
Reprinted by permission of The New American Library, Inc.,
New York. The quotation on page 18 copyright 1950 by John
Frederick Muehl. Reprinted from* Interview With India *by
John Frederick Muehl by permission of The John Day Company,
Inc., Publisher. The quotation on pages 81-82 from* Journey
Among Warriors, *by Eve Curie. Copyright © 1943 by Eve Curie.
Reprinted by permission of Doubleday and Company, Inc., and
Curtis Brown, Ltd. Quotations on pages 22, 23, 25, 26, 28, 30, 34,
35, 39, 43, and 45 from* The Story of My Experiments With
Truth, *by permission of Beacon Press, Boston, Massachusetts.
Quotations on pages 50 and 88 reprinted by permission of The
Macmillan Company from* Collected Poems and Plays of
Rabindranath Tagore, *copyright 1913, 1914, 1916, 1917, 1918,
1921, 1937 by The Macmillan Company, and by permission of
Macmillan and Co., Ltd., London.*

Contents

Salt March to the Sea

On the morning of March 12, 1930, a small, sinewy man wearing only sandals and a white loincloth picked up a long walking stick and began a march of 241 miles. The place was Sabarmati, India, and he marched south to the sea at Dandi. His name was Mohandas Karamchand Gandhi, but many called him the *Mahatma*, or the great soul. Others called him *Bapu*, meaning father, for he was recognized as the spiritual father of all India.

The little man who looked like a poor peasant was giving a signal to his countrymen that England would no longer be permitted to rule India against India's will. The country had been dominated by the British as a Crown Colony for more years than her people could remember. She ached to be free, but Britain would not let her go. Gandhi was destined to change the patterns of history, and he did so without raising a sword or lifting a gun.

As he walked, the sixty-one-year-old Gandhi was accompanied by seventy-eight men and women—*satyagrahis*—who shared his beliefs. He and his followers trekked along the winding dirt road from village to village for a period of twenty-four days. A land of over 400 million people turned its ears to catch the fall of each footstep. He was cheered as he came. People sprinkled the roads with water to hold down the dust, and they scattered leaves and flowers before him. Many fell to their knees as he passed.

By the time he reached the sea his group numbered several thousand. While the sea washed upon the shore, the group offered prayers. Then Gandhi did a strange thing. He walked into the warm waters and then returned to the shore. Thousands were watching him as he bent over and took a handful of salt that had been left on the sand by the waves.

With one simple gesture, Gandhi had broken the British law which made it a crime to possess salt that was not purchased from the government salt monopoly. Salt was one of the few things the poor people of India needed most of all for daily existence. The manufacture and sale of salt was one of the means by which Britain taxed India heavily.

Because he took a pinch of salt from the sea, Gandhi and several of his friends were sent to jail. He went cheerfully, for he knew that his gesture had set an example for all of India. He taught the unwashed masses that they could make their own salt in spite of the British. People marched in droves to the sea to take salt. Others made salt in pans on the roofs of their homes.

British rule had been defied and England felt the sting. As a result of the courageous act of Mahatma Gandhi, the sun was beginning to set on the British Union Jack that had stood firmly over India for so many years.

Gandhi takes a handful of salt from the sea, while his followers watch. In doing this, he was breaking the British salt laws which forbade Indians from obtaining salt from any source but the government monopoly.

11

India

What mold of man was he who could influence history? To understand Gandhi, one must first understand the land into which he was born and the people who were uplifted by his existence.

The great land body of India is located in South Central Asia and juts down like a great triangle into the warm waters of the Indian Ocean between the Arabian Sea and the Bay of Bengal. It is about two thirds the size of the United States and has a population of about 475 million people—more than the combined population of Russia and the United States.

Far in the northeast of India stand the mighty Himalayas, the tallest mountains in the world, home of the eternal snows. To the northwest stretch vast deserts. The southern peninsula is rimmed by low mountains called the Ghats. At the far southern tip lies the island of Ceylon.

Great rivers such as the Indus, the Brahmaputra, and the Ganges flow from the fertile northern plains, where much of India's vast population is concentrated, down to the sunlit sea. These rivers are considered holy places, where a devout person can cleanse his body and his soul. It is said that more than ten million people bathe each day in the Ganges.

Nearly one fifth of India is covered with jungle, the home of predatory animals such as the fierce Bengal tigers, the unpredictable hooded cobra, and the majestic Indian elephant.

India bends beneath the extremes of climate. Bitter cold grips the mountains in the north; unbearable heat oppresses the south. During the long summer months, when the temperatures sometimes reach 125 degrees Fahrenheit, the people in central and southern India vainly seek relief from the stagnant heat. Unless the monsoon winds come, bringing cool moisture and rains from the sea, millions of the poor in India desire nothing and do nothing. When the monsoon ceases, thousands of starving people sit in silence and wait patiently for death.

India is one of the oldest civilized lands in the world, with a culture that began more than 5000 years ago. During most of that time India was a world to herself, a world rich with poets, scholars, princes, doctors, mathematicians, and holy men—and poor with starving masses of people. Even to this day there are primitive people who live in caves and the hollows of trees, subsisting on honey and nuts, roots and herbs.

Though India is primarily an agricultural nation, thousands of skilled artisans have emerged over the centuries —men and women who have woven beautiful cloth, carved exquisite jewelry, and built magnificent temples. Twenty thousand men labored nearly twenty-five years to build the Taj Mahal at Agra, the most beautiful of India's temples.

Indian society evolved into a rigid system of social classes, or castes.

The ancient land of India—its high mountains, dense jungles, sacred rivers, and temples— and its gods of all sizes, shapes, and powers.

Among them were the Brahman priests, the soldiers, the merchants and farmers (Gandhi's caste), and the craftsmen. A large number of Indians, called Untouchables, had no caste at all. They were the oppressed classes who lived in the filthiest parts of the cities and did the lowliest work. They cleaned up refuse and removed dead animals and garbage. Untouchables were not permitted to touch any caste Hindu or anything a caste Hindu touched.

Writing emerged in India between 1000 B.C. and 500 B.C. and was jealously guarded by Brahman priests and clerks. The ancient sacred language of India is called Sanskrit, meaning pure, or perfect. It was prepared and refined by poets and priests and transmitted down the centuries in a more or less unchanged form. Sanskrit is one of the original languages in the family of languages known as Indo-European. Many English words can be traced to Sanskrit, such as *night, bind, genus, daughter*, and *divine*. What Latin was to the Roman Empire, Sanskrit was to India.

A great body of Sanskrit literature called the *Vedas* developed in India between 2000 and 500 B.C. The *Vedas* constitute India's holy book. They are comprised of poems, hymns, prayers, and philosophy dealing with the origin of the world and the history of India. The writers considered the nature of man and his soul; where he is born, how he lives, and where he is going.

The most famous writer of Sanskrit in ancient India was a man of low caste by the name of Kalidasa who rose to favor in the courts of the wealthy

A Hindu worshiping at the statue of Siva, generally known as the third of the great triad of Hindu gods. His name in Sanskrit means "happy," or "of good omen."

princes. Kalidasa was writing epic poems in northern India at the time the once great Roman Empire was crumbling beneath the awful advance of the barbarians.

Kalidasa wrote tales of the old gods and heroes—of Rama, Vishnu, Krishna, Kali, and Indra. He sang songs of beautiful women who wore jasmine flowers in their hair and golden bracelets on their ankles, praising them for their love and faithful devotion to their husbands. He wrote of the sacred river Ganges which fell from heaven like a flight of stairs let down for the sons of men. He wrote of all the beauty in the Himalayas —of the enchanting clouds, the rainbow bridges, and the terrible lightning; of the gorgeous peacocks lifting their plumes in a dance of dazzling colors; of the wild flowers that grew forever and the swans that swam serenely in the mountain lakes where the scent of musk is never lost.

The poems of Kalidasa remind one that India, in her ancient days, was a place of exceptional taste and unrivaled beauty.

The principal religion of India is Hinduism, although Buddhism, Islam, Sikhism, Zoroastrianism, and Jainism have exerted considerable influence. Using the *Vedas* as the holy word, Brahman priests taught that each man and woman is reborn again and again until he is purified. This process, which they believe happens to all forms of life including even animals and plants, is called reincarnation. A man's body dies, but his soul is reborn into a new body. An Indian guru, or teacher, may point

to a snake shedding its skin and say, "See, the snake casts its old body away but keeps on living. Man is the same as a snake. He throws his old body away and takes life in a new body."

The Brahmans taught that the conduct of each man's life must be determined by his hereditary caste. According to the *Vedas*, each person has an obligation known as *dharma*. He may not step beyond the boundaries of his caste without becoming an *outcaste*, a person exiled from his family and friends.

Hindus believe that a man's fate is determined by his deeds in his present life. This is called *karma*. If one does not behave properly as a Brahman, he may be reborn in his next life as an Untouchable. If an Untouchable lives the way he is supposed to live, he might be reborn as a Brahman.

By proper conduct through many reincarnations, a devout Hindu may eventually reach his final state— *Nirvana*—or the state of being free from rebirth. The cycles of life and death are complete, the soul is purified and becomes absorbed into the entire universe, becoming part of God, or *Brahma*.

Over many centuries, Hinduism degenerated into idol worship, preference for ceremony, and excessive superstition. Because the Brahman priests taught that all human life was an illusion, the distinctions between good and bad, slavery and freedom, corruption and betterment were never clear. Disease, poverty, starvation, ignorance, and human sacrifice bred in the poorer castes. People were not encouraged to better themselves.

For many centuries India was divided and ruled by rival sultans, princes, and maharajahs. From this vast mixture of peoples who inhabited India, about fifteen major languages developed, including Urdu, Bengali, Hindi, Pakistani, Punjabi, and Gujarati (Gandhi's native tongue). More than one hundred minor languages and about seven hundred dialects also came to be spoken. Independent states emerged, and India was described by the Indian poet Tagore as ". . . many countries packed in one geographical receptacle."

After the Portuguese sailor Vasco da Gama reached India in 1498, Europeans began to look upon India as the gem of the Orient. India was called the Land of Spices, "a country of inexhaustible riches!"

Portuguese, Dutch, French, and British ships sailed to India to obtain spices, nuts, cloth, perfume, and jewels. In those days spices were used for both seasoning and food preservation, and were very much in demand.

Columbus had announced to Spain that he would find a western route to India to simplify trade routes. Instead he discovered, by accident, the West Indies and America.

England was in her great period of mercantile and imperialistic expansion and "obsessed by the demon of commercial selfishness." She was gathering colonies throughout the world and India was a prime jewel, internally weak and potentially very wealthy.

Of all the European nations which occupied India, the British ruled most effectively. English merchants founded the East India Company in the early 1600's "to establish a large, well-groomed, sure English dominion in India for all time to come." Thus began a thorough and systematic exploitation of India's resources.

British rule brought an end to the internal warring of the princes, sultans, and maharajahs. The English imposed a vast system of civil service government across the body of India which tended to unite the various states and factions of India into one country.

British soldiers, British engineers, and British businessmen swarmed into India. They harnessed the rivers and diverted waters into the thirsting soils. They

In a ship something like this one, Vasco da Gama sailed to India for the first time in 1497. Trade routes were opened between India and Europe, and sailors from all over Europe went to India to obtain "exotic" spices and other goods.

16

modernized farming techniques and improved the distribution of goods. Engineers built roads, railroads, canals, hospitals, factories, and schools. The educated classes of India learned to speak the English language and began to unify under the discipline of Parliament and democratic ideals. Many Indians admired the English, who were taller, stronger, and better fed.

The coming of the British also placed a great burden on India. By promoting her own industries, Britain all but destroyed the native crafts and skills and the initiative of India's people. Peasants were forced to buy English goods and pay taxes to the English government in order to support the civil service in India and the exchequer in London. England taxed India heavily and constantly drained her wealth and resources. As England grew richer, India grew poorer.

The East was popularized in the West by the books of Rudyard Kipling, who was born in Bombay, India, in 1865—four years before the birth of Gandhi. Kipling was the son of an English civil servant who was curator of the museum at Lahore.

Kipling glamorized the British soldiers who guarded the Khyber Pass in northwest India. This pass had been the pathway of traders and invaders for thousands of years. Kipling also wrote poems and "ditties" about the British soldiers who fought in India.

Now in Injia's sunny clime
Where I used to spend my time
A-servin' of 'Er Majesty the Queen,
Of all them blackfaced crew
The finest man I knew
Was our regimental bhisti, Gunga Din.

He wrote the *Jungle Book*, a collection of fictional tales dealing with the struggle for animal survival and the balance of nature in the Indian jungles. And he wrote about the human struggle for survival in the Indian cities of Calcutta, Bombay, and Delhi. He described the bustling activity that took place in the crowded bazaars, where merchants sold their goods and moneylenders lent money at incredible rates of "7% a month with a mortgage on the unborn calf."

Kipling wrote in *Kim:*

All India is full of holy men
stammering gospels in strange
tongues; shaken and consumed
in the fires of their own zeal;
dreamers, babblers, visionaries:
as it had been from the
beginning and will continue
to the end.

The India of today is not much different from what it was in Kipling's day. There is still a vast confusion of peoples. Greedy landlords and moneylenders take advantage of the poor. Travelers tell with astonishment of the people who sleep side by side on the pavements of the city streets or on the platforms of the railroad stations all night long. When they arise in the morning, they are wearing everything they own in the world.

Worse than that are the conditions in India's 700,000 villages. The peasants —or *ryots*—live in squalid ignorance. Their lives emerge and decay within the vicinity of small, isolated communities that serve about fifty to one hundred families. Until recently, the average lifespan of an Indian was a mere twenty-six years.

Filth and garbage are littered everywhere in the villages. Diseased cattle roam about freely. Exposed sewage, with its swarm of insects, runs along narrow alleys where villagers and cows pass continually. One American traveler wrote, "The smells rose too, smells of spice and urine, of garlic and curry powder and dysentery stools, all the assorted smells of the Indian village, all the smells of life, decay, and death."

The water is contaminated and sanitary conditions are utterly lacking; the food is not adequate to prevent malnutrition, and disease breeds more disease. The peasants are unclean and do nothing to change their conditions. Only by the constant prodding of men like Gandhi and the policies of the government have they been urged to better their conditions at all. And even that they resent.

These English engineers
are building a dredge which
will be used to deepen
canals, as part of Britain's
efforts to industrialize
India.

Gandhi the Boy

Mohandas Karamchand Gandhi was born on October 2, 1869, in Porbandar, India, a small town on the west coast between Bombay and Karachi. This town near the Arabian Sea was a town of narrow lanes, crowded bazaars, and white stone buildings that glistened brightly in the sun.

Gandhi's family were Hindus who belonged to the merchant and grocer caste, but his grandfather, father, and uncles rose to political office as *diwans*, or chief ministers, of their small states.

His father, Karamchand Gandhi, married four times. Mohandas was the youngest of four children born to his father by his last wife, Putlibai.

Gandhi's father, from all accounts, was a generous man, but short-tempered. His mother was a deeply religious woman, who recited to her children verses from the *Bhagavad Gita*, a Hindu devotional book, and from the *Ramayana*, a Hindu epic poem.

There was little to distinguish Gandhi's boyhood. He was shy and withdrawn and, by his own admission, a mediocre student. He attended a grammar school at which, for lack of writing materials, the alphabet lessons were written with fingers in the dust.

When Mohandas was seven years old, his family moved to the city of Rajkot, which was more prosperous and had better schools than Porbandar.

Gandhi's family arranged for his marriage when he was a boy of only thirteen. This was the customary manner in which marriages were contracted between Hindu families. The prospective bride and groom had nothing to say about it, and the marriage was usually a matter of economic convenience between families of the same caste. Sometimes several of these childhood weddings took place at the same time, and were occasions for great confusion and celebration.

An exterior view of the house in which Gandhi was said to have been born on October 2, 1869.

Gandhi's bride, also thirteen, was an illiterate girl named Kasturbai. Mohandas quickly assumed the authority of a husband, even though he was greatly frightened by his new role in life. At that young age, he was totally unprepared to deal with marriage, and at times was petty, severe, jealous, and quarrelsome. Kasturbai remained a faithful wife throughout her life. Gandhi taught her how to read and write, and she helped him advance his purpose in the world. She bore him four sons.

By the time Gandhi was in high school, his fellow students thought of him as a serious-minded boy. In his classes, which were taught in English, he studied Sanskrit, geometry, chemistry, and Persian. He never learned to spell very well, but always strived for self-improvement. India's great books impressed him very much. He admired those mythical heroes who dedicated their lives to conducting themselves in a decent manner, helping their fellow man, and pursuing truth unswervingly.

He did not enjoy gymnastics, cricket, or football while he was in school, but he did acquire the habit of taking long walks for exercise, a habit which continued throughout his entire life.

As a withdrawn, reflective boy, Gandhi had few friends. There was one lad, however, who excelled in physical sports whom Gandhi admired for his daring boldness and strength. They became close friends and the stronger boy exercised considerable influence on the young Mohandas.

This lad convinced Gandhi that " the English are able to rule over us because they are meat eaters, and I am stronger than you because I am a meat eater. India needs reform. If the whole country took to eating meat the English would be overcome and we would rule our own country."

The logic appealed to Gandhi, for he was often the victim of irrational fears and wished that he were stronger. He wrote in his autobiography, "I was a coward . . . haunted by the fear of thieves, ghosts and serpents. I did not dare to stir out of doors at night . . . it was almost impossible for me to sleep in the dark, as I would imagine ghosts coming from one direction, thieves from another and serpents from a third. I could not bear to sleep without a light in the room. How could I bear to disclose my fears to my wife sleeping at my side?"

So, to acquire strength, Gandhi went with his courageous friend to a lonely spot by the river and ate meat. Unfortunately, it was very tough goat meat. He became sick instantly and felt very guilty because his parents had told him that good Hindus do not eat meat. That evening he had a horrible nightmare, which he felt to be a punishment. "Everytime I dropped off to sleep," recalled Gandhi, "it would seem as though a live goat were bleating inside me, and I would jump up full of remorse." That experience put an end to Gandhi's meat-eating adventures and he remained a vegetarian the rest of his life.

Like other boys his own age, Gandhi took to smoking stumps of cigarettes and creating minor mischief. On one

Gandhi at age 17.

occasion, he stole pennies from the house servant in order to buy cigarettes. This made him feel so guilty that he wrote a letter confessing the whole affair to his father and pledged never to steal again.

His father was very understanding about the incident and did not punish the boy. This gave Gandhi his first lesson in *ahimsa*, which is a Sanskrit concept of feeling love and of doing no harm to any living creature—in other words, nonviolence. Gandhi was so impressed by his father's attitude that he adopted *ahimsa* as his personal creed and maintained it for the rest of his life.

In those days, when he was in high school, Gandhi mingled freely with Hindus, Moslems, and Zoroastrians, and learned to respect all religions. He never believed that Hinduism was the only true religion, but rather that there were good things to be learned from all faiths.

The English, of course, were Christians, and Gandhi had some misgivings about them. "Only Christianity at that time was an exception. I developed a sort of dislike for it. . . . In those days Christian missionaries used to stand near the high school pouring abuse on Hindus and their gods. I could not endure this."

When he was a mature man he would say, "All religions are true, and all religions have some error in them . . . I am a Hindu, a Moslem, a Christian and a Jew . . . I want the cultures of all lands to be blown about my house as freely as possible. But I refuse to be blown off my feet."

23

Law School in London

Following graduation from high school, Gandhi attended a local college, but did not do well. He was eighteen, and his family expected him to choose a profession. Though medicine interested him, he was finally convinced that he should study law. An older brother was to finance his education. Since the best place to study law was in London, and many well-to-do Indians went there to further their education, Gandhi settled on a school there. He set sail for England in 1888.

When he arrived, he found boarding rooms in a poor section of London and enrolled at the Inner Temple, one of four London law schools known as the Inns of Court. His first feelings were of nostalgia for his wife, who had remained at home, for his mother, and for India. "Everything was strange—the people, their ways, and even their dwellings. I was a complete novice on the matter of English etiquette and continually had to be on my guard."

The hopeful scholar attempted to become an English gentleman, expecting that in this way he would be brought "into key with the dominant note in British life." Gandhi, dressed in Bond Street clothes, must have looked somewhat ludicrous—a skinny, dark-skinned boy whose ears stuck out, dressed in a necktie and stiff collar.

Besides his law courses, Gandhi took lessons in French, dancing, and elocution. Since he could not follow the rhythm of the music, he had to give up dancing. He next tried the violin, but that, too, proved difficult for him to learn. He apparently had no musical talent whatever.

He took the time to learn Latin because it was useful in understanding lawbooks. Latin also provided him with the necessary background for a much greater command of the English language.

Law students customarily attended a great number of dinners at which they met other students, heard lectures, and discussed current events. Though Gandhi went to these dinners, he had never learned to express himself well in conversation. As a result he restrained his thoughts. He later wrote, "Proneness to exaggerate, to suppress or modify the truth is a natural weakness

Gandhi as a law student in London.

25

of man, and silence is necessary in order to surmount it. A man of few words will rarely be thoughtless in his speech; he will measure every word."

Gandhi further restricted his already meager diet after he joined London's Vegetarian Society. He refused to eat any kind of flesh from birds, fish, or animals. He even gave up eggs, and never touched alcoholic beverages.

At that time Gandhi's wide reading included the works of Tolstoy and Carlyle, the poems of Shelley, and the Bible. He especially enjoyed the New Testament, and it excited in him an admiration for Jesus. He said that the Sermon on the Mount, in which Jesus gave his blessing to the poor, the meek, the merciful, and the peacemakers, went straight to his heart. It reminded him of a previous saying in the *Bhagavad Gita*: "He is the help of the helpless, the strength of the weak." Jesus' love for his fellow men delighted Gandhi beyond measure.

While he was at law school in London, Gandhi's religious attitudes became more defined. As he had throughout his entire life, he prayed every morning and every evening. This was his way of sorting out and redefining his purpose in life, of sharing the sufferings of his fellow men, and of admitting to himself his own weaknesses. He found refuge from his loneliness and homesickness in prayer and introspection. Sometimes prayer required no conscious thought at all, only silent awareness. He was later to write that "supplication, worship, prayer are not superstitious. They are acts more real than the acts of eating, drinking, sitting or walking. Although prayer springs from the purity of the heart, prayer needs no speech. It is in itself independent of any sensuous effort . . . an unfailing means of cleansing the heart of passions."

In June of 1891, at the end of three years study in England, Mohandas Gandhi passed his examinations in Roman and Common Law and was called to the bar. The day after he was admitted to the bar, he set sail for India and home. Several unfortunate experiences lay in wait for the young barrister.

A ship entering Bombay harbor in 1891. It was at this time that Gandhi returned to India to practice law after being admitted to the bar in England.

Inauspicious Beginning

Gandhi was eager to be reunited with his wife and family. He was deeply saddened on his arrival, however, when he learned that his mother had died while he was in England. His older brother had not written him about it for fear that it might have disrupted his education.

With the help of his brother, Gandhi opened up his first law offices in Bombay. He knew nothing of Hindu or Moslem law and was poorly prepared to be a practical barrister in his homeland. He discovered soon enough that knowledge of lawbooks had little to do with the practice of law. He realized that cases were bought and sold for favors and commissions.

The dubious activity in the courts dismayed him. He noticed that many lawyers behaved in cunning, devious ways; that some men solicited and accepted bribes in order to allow defendants to escape prosecution of the law; that petty politicians could throw their weight around and influence decisions of the bench; and that many judges were not alert to the true merits of a case. What did the law mean by justice? The high ideals of justice seemed to be systematically disregarded in the courtroom. Now Gandhi knew what his fellow students had meant when they talked about the "liar's profession."

Regrettably, Gandhi was not even sure how to apply the points of law to specific cases of property, where the use of one man's property infringed upon the rights of another man.

His first case in court was a disaster. He tried to defend the property rights of his client, but he could not gather the courage to cross-examine the witnesses. "I stood up," he recalled, "but my heart sank into my boots. My head was reeling and I felt as though the whole court was doing likewise. I could think of no question to ask!"

Indentured Indian laborers working in the mines of South Africa. After their term of five years, these laborers often stayed in Africa to live as free men.

Because of this embarrassing experience, Gandhi returned his client's fee, and refused to take further cases that involved either prosecution or defense in court. He drafted a few contracts and wills, but could not earn a decent living either in Bombay or his hometown of Rajkot. He grew restless and began looking to new horizons.

In those years, many Moslems, Hindus, and Parsis (Zoroastrians from Bombay) were emigrating to South Africa, where they worked as indentured laborers in the mines or on British-owned sugar, tea, and coffee plantations. Ordinarily, an indentured laborer sold his services to an employer for a period of five years. The employer paid for his transportation to and from South Africa, and paid him a modest wage.

These indentured workers had been arriving in South Africa since 1860. After completing their five years of service, many of them decided to stay on and live as free men. They worked hard and were thrifty. Others joined them from India and started small stores, farms, and businesses. As the free indentures became more and more involved in commercial activity, they needed help to protect their property rights and their business interests.

A successful Moslem firm contacted Gandhi and asked him if he would work for them in South Africa, helping them with their business and legal affairs. Gandhi decided to try his luck in South Africa for one year, and sailed for Natal, again leaving his wife and family at home. He could not foresee that he would stay twenty years and become the foremost guardian of Indian rights in a foreign country.

The Struggle Begins

In 1893, Gandhi arrived in South Africa, a country that had been colonized by Dutch farmers, who were called Boers, and by the English. Many of these European settlers grew jealous of Indians who acquired property or businesses. The Boers, who lived primarily in the Orange Free State, would not allow free Indians to own property, start businesses, or farm. The laws and courts favored the interests of the Europeans, and the Dutch lawbooks inhumanly referred to Indians as "semi-barbarous Asiatics." Even today, the African Dutch are responsible for enforcing the system of apartheid, which strips nonwhites of property and voting rights.

The darker-skinned Indians, whose religion was strange to the Christian Europeans, were often treated with contempt. White people called them "coolies" regardless of their education, and forced them to travel third class and stay in cheap hotels regardless of their wealth. Under such conditions, the Indians could not expect to be comfortable.

Gandhi's legal affairs immediately threw him into the midst of this racial bitterness. When he traveled to the cities of Praetoria, Charlestown, Johannesburg, and Durban, he was frequently insulted and even beaten severely. He had never witnessed anything so cruel in either England or India. He stated at the time, "It has always been a mystery to me how men can feel themselves honored by the humiliation of their fellow beings."

Gandhi vowed to fight for fair treatment for minority races in South Africa; he first tried political means. He made speeches to his fellow Indians. He called for them to be fair and truthful in their business relations; he urged them to develop better sanitary habits; he told them to forget religious and caste differences; and he led them in the formation of an organization to defend and protect Indian rights—the Natal Indian Congress. He opposed the excessive poll tax designed by the English to discourage Indians from setting up businesses and competing with the Europeans on equal terms. His political experiences led Gandhi to believe that his life was not destined for personal gain but rather for the public good.

Shortly after the Natal Indian Congress had been formed, an indentured laborer named Balasundaram came to Gandhi's law offices. The man had been indentured to a wealthy European resident of Durban.

Balasundaram was in a wretched state. His clothes were torn, his two front teeth broken, and his mouth bleeding. His master had lost his temper and beat Balasundaram mercilessly. He stood before Gandhi, weeping, and asked for help. Further beatings would be too much to endure.

In those days, an indentured laborer had about the same rights a slave would have had—none. He was considered the property of his employer, and no one really cared what a master did to his workers.

Gandhi was appalled. After having a white doctor treat Balasundaram's wounds, Gandhi called on Balasundaram's employer. He asked the man if he would be willing to release Balasundaram to the custody of another employer. The master, only too happy to get rid of his troublesome indenture, agreed to the transfer. Thus, Gandhi was able to prevent further abuse to a poor laborer.

The news traveled fast. Poor indentures, who lived and worked almost in a state of semi-slavery, heard of this man named Gandhi—a barrister—who was willing to care for and defend an indentured laborer. The story traveled back on ships to southern India. Immigrants, waiting to go to South Africa, heard the news that there was a man named Gandhi who was their friend.

Gandhi became popular overnight, and was the champion of hordes of indentures. They filled his office with their grievances and hopes.

The young attorney had a way of making friends wherever he went, for his sincere and tolerant manner attracted many admirers, and his sense of humor and goodwill disarmed his critics. Among his friends were many of the Christian missionaries who came to South Africa as doctors, nurses, and teachers. Most of these missionaries had good intentions, but their zealous en-

thusiasm created ill feelings when they informed Hindus and Moslems that their age-old religious beliefs were in error.

Christian missionaries assumed that all men were sinful, and that non-Christians were somehow more sinful than Christians. They felt it was their duty to convert the "heathens" and deliver them to Jesus for forgiveness and ultimate salvation.

Since the Christians were the wealthiest and most powerful people in South Africa, they received many converts.

Gandhi, however, was not easily influenced, even by his friends among the Christian community. He admired Jesus, but believed that God had many voices, not just one.

Furthermore, Gandhi wanted more than the forgiveness of sins. He wanted to see sin itself eliminated. "Hate the sin, but not the sinner," was his creed. Forty years later he was to tell his countrymen, "Hate the British system, but not the British."

One friendly missionary accused Gandhi of being superstitious. Gandhi

Christian missionaries in a South African marketplace. Though Gandhi had many Christian friends, they could never convince him to convert to Christianity.

33

had been wearing a string of Hindu beads around his neck that had been given to him by his mother.

The missionary thought Gandhi should get rid of the beads and told him, "Mr. Gandhi, let me break the necklace."

Gandhi replied, "No, it is a sacred gift from my mother."

Then the missionary asked, "But don't you believe in it?"

Gandhi's answer was, "I do not know its mysterious significance. I do not think I should come to harm if I do not wear it. But I cannot, without sufficient reason, give up the necklace that my mother put around my neck out of love and in the conviction that it would be beneficial to my welfare. When, in the passage of time, it wears away and breaks of its own accord, I shall have no desire to get a new one. But this necklace cannot be broken."

Gandhi and the Christian missionary discussing Gandhi's beads. Gandhi refused to break the necklace not because he felt it had a religious significance, but because it had been a gift from his mother.

The young attorney wanted to be kind to his new Christian friends and was willing to attend Wesleyan church services with them. He enjoyed singing the hymns, but the rest of the service did not make a favorable impression on him. He wrote in his autobiography, "They were not an assembly of devout souls; they appeared rather to be worldly-minded people, going to church for recreation and in conformity to custom."

The sermons were dull, and Gandhi frequently found himself dozing off. He was not ashamed about this, however, because many of his Christian neighbors were doing the same thing.

In 1896, after three years of concentrated effort in South Africa to improve the situation of the Indians there, Gandhi decided to take a leave of absence. He went home to India to get his family. As soon as he arrived, he began to write a pamphlet describing the unfortunate conditions of Indian people in South Africa. After a month of preparation, hundreds of copies were ready to be distributed to important officials throughout India. Traveling from city to city, Gandhi lectured about the need for fair treatment of Indians abroad.

During this stay in India, Gandhi was introduced to important members of the Indian National Congress Party, an organization interested in achieving India's independence from England. They urged him to stay in India to help free the country from the burdens of what the Indians called British Raj (British Rule). Gandhi, however, still considered himself a loyal British citizen and was not ready to resist the British in India. Besides, he was anxious to return to South Africa, for there was important work to be done there.

Voice of Dissent

After a stay of six months, Gandhi again sailed for South Africa, this time taking with him his wife, his nephew, and his two sons. Two other boys would be born to him and Kasturbai in a foreign land. During the trip, Gandhi's ship was thrown into the jaws of a storm. Most of the passengers were so frightened that they prayed for their lives.

Gandhi was everywhere, helping the sick and the frightened and transmitting messages from the captain to the passengers until the sea subsided.

That storm was not so terrifying as the one waiting for him at Natal. When the ship arrived at Durban, it was placed in quarantine on the pretense that it was carrying plague germs from Bombay. The real reason for the quarantine was that the white citizens of Durban did not want Gandhi to land. They thought of him as a troublemaker and charged that he had said false things about the white people of Natal. They also claimed that he was bringing shiploads of Indian settlers to flood the land.

Threats were sent out to the ship saying that Gandhi would be thrown overboard unless he and his people returned to India. The ship was held in quarantine for twenty-three days before being allowed to enter the harbor. When the passengers debarked, an inflamed crowd was waiting for Gandhi. Stones and rotten eggs were thrown at him and

Gandhi and his wife Kasturbai. At about the time this photograph was taken, Gandhi returned to South Africa, bringing his wife, his nephew, and his two sons. He had just spent six months in India, but felt he was more needed in Africa.

he was kicked to the ground. Fortunately, the wife of the police commissioner came to his rescue and fended off the mob, using her umbrella. Since they feared her husband, they withdrew, and Gandhi was saved from further beatings. The crowd was so angry that Gandhi received police protection for a few days. At least one intended lynching was prevented.

Gandhi refused to prosecute his assailants. He felt that after they calmed down they would realize their mistake. He thus put to use an old Sanskrit saying: "Forgiveness is the decoration of the brave."

The demand for Gandhi's legal services increased after he was resettled in South Africa with his family. Many people trusted him, and his earnings were between twenty-five and thirty thousand dollars a year. The money he did not need for his basic family needs he donated to public causes. He was becoming more eager for humanitarian work and volunteered for service in a small hospital.

The years between 1899 and 1902 saw the emergence of the South African War, more commonly known as the Boer War. The Dutch Boers were a fiercely independent people, whose main occupation was farming. The Dutch resented the British commercial interests encroaching on their lands. British mining interests were eating up territory in the Transvaal and Orange Free State, and the Dutch tried various methods to stop them. They refused to grant citizenship to English settlers and imposed excessive taxes on English businesses. These measures led to war between the British and the Boers, for, of course, England felt it necessary to protect her commercial interests.

England, because of her greater number of forces, eventually won the war, which was hard fought on both sides. The English were lenient in their terms to the Boers. The Dutch territories were annexed by the British Crown, and the Union of South Africa was formed, with the Dutch and English states as independent members. English statesmen knew that a victor would not be able to establish good business or political relations with a former rival whom they forced to pay heavily for defeat in war.

During the Boer War Gandhi continued to show his loyalty to the British. He organized and led an Indian corps of stretcher-bearers and medical aides who tended the wounded on the battlefield and carried them off to hospitals at British bases while under the fire of enemy guns.

Louis Fischer, Gandhi's famous biographer, wrote that Gandhi "wore a khaki uniform, a jaunty, broad-brimmed cowboy felt hat, a Red Cross armband, and a drooping mustache."

A witness to the war recalled, "After a night's work which had shattered men with bigger frames, I came across Gandhi in the early morning sitting by the roadside eating a regulation army biscuit. Every man was dull and depressed, and damnation was invoked on everything. But Gandhi was stoical in his bearing, cheerful, and confident in his conversations, and had a kindly eye. He did one good!"

The rebellion of the Zulus against the English broke out in 1906. During that "British Manhunt," Gandhi carried off as many wounded as he could, no matter which side they fought on.

For services rendered in both conflicts, Gandhi and his comrades received war medals from the British. At that time, Gandhi was under the belief that the British Empire existed for the welfare of the world. Years later, he would change his mind and return the medals.

Gandhi was thrifty with time and made his remaining years in South Africa very productive, tending to the demands of his law practice, taking care of his family and friends, and devoting long hours to reading and meditation. He considered the *Bhagavad Gita*, India's great epic poem, his "infallible guide of human conduct." The *Gita* stressed that it was not necessary for a mortal to possess material things and great wealth in order to be happy. Even though a man may exercise control over vast possessions, he must never consider them his own. His role is that of temporary guardian of the gifts of God, gifts to be shared with all for the benefit of mankind.

Many South African laws were oppressive and unfair to Indians, just as there have been laws in the United States unfair and insulting to American Negroes. Indians in South Africa were not permitted to use first-class public accommodations on trains, coaches, or at hotels. These were reserved exclusively for white Europeans. Asiatics and Negroes were not allowed freedom of movement from place to place, though Europeans could go anywhere they wished. Even the schools were off limits to Indians and their property rights were considered invalid. Nonetheless, Indians were taxed at a higher rate than were the Europeans in order to support the will and treasury of the British government that ruled them.

In order to complicate racial matters further, the English courts issued a prejudicial law stating that only Christian marriages were legal. Overnight, Hindu, Moslem, and Parsi wedding ceremonies were declared unlawful— even though they were part of ancient religious traditions. This incredible court action automatically reduced all Indian wives to the status of concubines, stripped families of legal protection, and caused much confusion and resentment.

These were the kinds of unfair laws and deplorable conditions that Gandhi wanted to change. In order to express his views to the entire community of Indians in South Africa, he founded his own newspaper, *Indian Opinion*. He wrote and edited most of it and published it in both English and Gujarati, his native language.

In spite of pressing political needs, Gandhi would always drop everything in order to nurse the sick. When an outbreak of plague threatened to decimate the Indian population in Johannesburg, the stricken had to be quarantined in a large warehouse. Most people were

afraid to help them for fear of being exposed to the disease.

Gandhi and several assistants rushed to the scene and helped the sick until the plague subsided. Gandhi seemed to have unusual immunity to contagious diseases, which he believed was due to proper habits of cleanliness and a very light diet. His medical attention on many occasions was of great comfort to the sick. The grateful Indian population began to call him "Bhai," meaning brother.

Gandhi was instrumental in founding two community settlements for the benefit of Indian people in South Africa —the Phoenix Settlement, and the Tolstoy Farm. Within the confines of these farms, groups of Indians lived together. Work was divided among the men, the women, and the children. They made clothes, cultivated the land, and even did typesetting for Gandhi's newspaper. Gandhi gave much of his own time to the education of the children— reading, writing, geography, history, mathematics, and religion. He invited European friends to live on the farms, and many came.

Let it not be said that Gandhi was a man without fault. His political activities frequently interfered with his family life. Even though he was concerned with the moral character of his four sons and their proper behavior, he never provided them with an education equal to his own. Nor did he provide much for them in the way of material comfort or worldly possessions.

His sons tended to resent him because they were not trained to compete in the world in any profession. His oldest boy, Harilal, became an alcoholic. Harilal converted to the Moslem religion, changed his name to Abdulla, and wrote articles for newspapers that were highly critical of his father. The other boys, Manilal, Ramdas, and Devadas, were more faithful to the family.

Gandhi, who had a tendency to trust everyone, was sometimes gullible. At one time, a fast-talking American salesman in South Africa sold Gandhi a life insurance policy. The salesman informed Gandhi that in America it was

Gandhi (center) and some friends outside his law offices in Durban, Natal. While in Durban, Gandhi worked very hard to raise the prestige of the Indian community.

considered a religious obligation to be insured, and that it was therefore Gandhi's religious duty to be insured for the benefit of his wife and children.

After Gandhi paid for the policy, he had second thoughts. He asked himself, "Why should I assume that death would claim me earlier than others? In getting my life insured, have I robbed my wife and children of their self-reliance? Why should I not be like one of them?" Gandhi let his policy elapse.

Like Albert Schweitzer, Gandhi wanted to see no harm done to life in any form. That was the true meaning of *ahimsa*. On one brief trip to India, while he was traveling from city to city learning more about the problems India faced under British rule, he was witness to the wholesale slaughter of sheep in the state of Bengal. He and his traveling companions encountered a stream of sheep being sacrificed to the ancient Indian goddess Kali. Gandhi detested what he saw. The poor animals were dying in a bath of blood. He told his companions,

"To my mind the life of a lamb is no less precious than that of a human being. I hold that, the more helpless a creature, the more entitled it is to protection by man from the cruelty of man."

Even as he watched the sheep being led to slaughter, he was able to muse on how the British were leading the Indians like sheep; how the British were masters and the Indians slaves. The British believed that their rule was good for their Crown Colonies, even though some of their administrators abroad were petty, greedy men.

Gandhi began to see how a lack of independence could crush the human spirit. He was reminded by one of his companions that "As the elephant is powerless to think in terms of the ant, in spite of the best intentions in the world, even so is the Englishman powerless to think in terms of, or legislate for, the Indian." Gandhi knew that his help was needed in India, but he was not yet finished with his work in South Africa.

Sheep being led to slaughter in India. Gandhi compared this action with the actions of the British toward the Indians, and saw how the human spirit could be crushed if it had no independence.

43

Passive Resistance

South Africa was the birthplace of moral convictions that were to remain with Gandhi for the rest of his life. At times, he was very short tempered with his wife, Kasturbai. He once tried to throw her out of the house because she refused to wash a pan that had been touched by a member of the Untouchable caste who had been a guest in the house.

Gandhi would have no part of this behavior, and refused to honor caste obligations that were inconsiderate of people from lower castes. He was very angry with Kasturbai. But when his wife was outside the gate, she reminded him that she had no other place to go in the world. Gandhi felt very guilty about his cruel display of temper and brought Kasturbai back into the house. This incident caused him to begin thinking seriously about ways to control his base emotions. He eventually decided there was only one way—a way that had been used by many holy men throughout the

history of India. It was called the vow of *Brahmacharya.*

Brahmacharya literally means "search after Brahma," or search after God. Gandhi took this vow—a personal commitment to himself—in order to acquire the self-restraint which he deemed necessary for the life of a highly devoted public servant. The person who took the vow of Brahmacharya was attempting to purify his body and his mind. His aim was to have control of all his senses at all times. It involved giving up many material cares for the world and the family, and turning the mind toward spiritual ends.

Brahmacharya is somewhat like the vow that a Roman Catholic priest or monk takes when he decides to live as a celibate for the good of the church. In accordance with his vow, the highly energetic Gandhi began living a very austere life, trying to avoid anything that might stimulate any of his senses and refrained from sexual relations with

his wife. He adhered to a stricter diet of only fruit, nuts, and goat's milk, and developed the habit of fasting.

Fasting, for Gandhi, meant that he would eat no food at all for certain periods of time. This was to become a very important technique by which the religious Gandhi was able to influence political ends. He even attempted to "fast to death" several times after he had become India's spiritual leader. These fasts shocked the nation into moral victories.

Besides serving as a political tool for truth, fasting deepened Gandhi's religious nature. He once stated, "What the eyes are for the outer world, fasts are for the inner."

Toward the end of his life he looked back upon his strict religious habits and said, "Life without Brahmacharya appears to me to be insipid and animal-like. The brute by nature knows no self-restraint. Man is man because he is capable of, and only insofar as he exercises, self-restraint."

The number of Gandhi's followers began to increase at a rapid pace. Poor people believed in him; educated people were inspired by him. Those who were his co-workers, committed to improving the social and political conditions for Indians, were called *satyagrahis*. The term *satyagraha* means "holding to the truth" or "truth force." Satyagraha became synonymous with Gandhi's struggle for truth in a world that was clouded with illusions and crowded with political mistakes. The true satyagrahi must be loyal to his aims and firm to his cause.

The force of truth, Gandhi felt, was not enough. The sword of satyagraha must be tempered with *ahimsa* or love. All those who strived for equal political rights must do no harm or injury to their enemies. Gandhi insisted above all on nonviolence.

45

Satyagraha had its origin with Gandhi's political activities in South Africa. But the idea quickly spread to India and the rest of the world. India would feel the keen edge of a sword that dropped no blood, and the world would learn of satyagraha as a vital political force. They called it "passive resistance" or "nonviolent resistance." Gandhi said, "Passive resistance is an all-sided sword . . . it never rusts and cannot be stolen." He called his satyagrahis "soldiers of peace," who fought to free India by nonviolent means from the grips of the British Lion.

The works of two American writers, Ralph Waldo Emerson and Henry David Thoreau, influenced the rising young barrister. He read them with keen interest. Thoreau's essay *Civil Disobedience* helped convince Gandhi of each man's right to disobey unfair, oppressive, and prejudicial laws. Laws that are not administered impartially throw men under tyranny. Tyranny is the precursor of civil war.

Gandhi went one step further: if the government enforces wicked laws and a conscientious citizen disobeys them, then he must be prepared to face the punishment—with no malice in his heart. Such situations were to arise many times in Gandhi's political career.

The Asiatic Registration Act of 1907 required all Indians to register with the local government, be fingerprinted like criminals, and carry special identifica-

Gandhi in a South African jail. He was imprisoned three times in one year for his acts of civil disobedience, and would eventually spend more than seven years in various jails as a political prisoner.

tion cards with them at all times. Since none of the European citizens had to do this, the law was very insulting to the Indians.

Gandhi attempted to get this law repealed, but the British officials would not pay attention to him. Finally, Gandhi stood up in a theater in Johannesburg before 3000 of his fellow countrymen and, in a high-pitched, cracking voice, urged them to disobey the law. All 3000 vowed not to register. They had had enough of the British oppression.

This was an act of civil disobedience. Gandhi and many other Indians were sent to jail. When he was released, Gandhi would not rest until this and other unfair laws crippling Indian people were stricken from existence.

Gandhi assembled peaceful protest marches and organized strikes among laborers in the mines. He was jailed again—three times in one year. He could hardly know that he was going to have to spend well over seven years in jails for his future political activities.

After several years of civil disobedience and nonviolent political agitation by the Indians, the British had had enough. The Indian Relief Bill was drawn up and submitted to the Union of South Africa Parliament.

The bill, which was adopted in 1914, did away with the excessive taxes imposed on Indian indentured laborers and cancelled all back taxes. Hindu, Moslem, and Parsi marriages were declared lawful. Indians were given more freedom to move from place to place. All men were to be considered free and equal under the law, and wives still in India were permitted to join their husbands in South Africa.

Gandhi himself had submitted this bill to the parliament in collaboration with General Smuts, the British governor of South Africa who had put him in jail several times. Smuts had been under great pressure to enforce an unpopular law. However, he admired Gandhi greatly. In a gesture of friendship, Gandhi sent General Smuts a pair of leather sandals he had made while in prison. The General wore them for many years and returned them to Gandhi in 1939 with gratitude.

Smuts recalled in a later document that Gandhi never lost his temper in political confrontations; he never felt resentment toward his oppressors and jailers; and he always kept up a pleasant smile and good spirits in the most trying situations.

Gandhi left South Africa at the age of forty-five, never to return. Material possessions that he had accumulated over twenty years were left to his friends and co-workers. He left because a distant drum was calling him home—his motherland was struggling for *Hind Swaraj*—India Home Rule. But first, he would return to England to serve the British flag once more.

The Poet and the Politician

World War I broke out in 1914, just before Gandhi and his wife arrived in England. The great powers of Germany, France, and England were in conflict over territorial influence in China and Africa. Japan, Russia, and Belgium joined England and France. Austria-Hungary fought with Germany. The United States eventually went to the aid of Great Britain in "the war to end all wars."

European powers were fiercely engaged in competition to acquire new colonies. Many nation-states were trying to take more territory for themselves by imperialistic expansion. The machines of war brought terrible destruction to all of Europe. Death and suffering were everywhere; soldiers lay side by side against the "silent slain" on Europe's ghastly battlefields.

Gandhi by this time was a self-declared pacifist. However, since he considered himself a British citizen who enjoyed the protection of the British Empire, he felt it was his duty to serve England during the war.

"I discovered," said Gandhi, "that the British Empire had certain ideals with which I have fallen in love, and one of those ideals is that every subject of the British Empire has the freest scope possible for his energy and honor. . . . I have more than once said that that government is best which governs least. I have found that it is possible for me to be governed least under the British Empire."

In London, he helped to organize an Indian ambulance and nursing corps to care for the wounded. He even worked with women making clothes for soldiers. In a sense, he was compromising his pacifism, and he had divided feelings about it. "Even those who confine themselves to attending the wounded in battle," he said, "cannot be absolved from the guilt of war."

While Gandhi was in England during World War I, he worked to organize an ambulance and nursing corps made up of Indians. Though he was a pacifist, he still considered himself a British citizen and felt obligated to help England during the war.

Only six months after he had arrived in England from South Africa, Gandhi became very ill and was forced to go home to India where he could rest and recuperate.

The tireless Gandhi spent little time looking after himself, but soon began to apply what he had learned in South Africa to the political problems of India. The job of lifting India from the state of political slavery to that of a free and independent country was a colossal, nearly impossible, undertaking. India seemed too vast in its area, too diverse in its population. It was not one country, but many.

Rabindranath Tagore, India's Nobel Prize-winning poet, observed the way the British ruled India, and wrote, "Here was a new impersonal empire, where the rulers were over us but not among us, who owned our land but could never belong to it."

Great India lay in servitude to the British, and many Indian people refused to shake the chains. Tagore told the story shown at the right that described India as her own prisoner.

Gandhi understood Tagore's allegory all too well. "Some Englishmen state that they took and hold India by the sword," he wrote. "Both statements are wrong. The sword is entirely useless for holding India. We alone keep them. . . . We like their commerce; they please us by their subtle methods and get what they want from us. . . . We further strengthen their hold by quarreling amongst ourselves."

With extreme patience, Gandhi sawed at that prisoner's chain with the tools of *satyagraha* and *ahimsa*.

Tagore had traveled through Japan, China, Europe, and the United States. He lectured to many people about India. He returned to India to bring home much of what he learned from the West. Gandhi and Tagore became close friends. It was Tagore who named Gandhi the Mahatma—the great soul.

Tagore saw India as "the eternal rag-picker at other people's dustbins." Gandhi saw India as a country of despised poor and starving masses who must be uplifted. Tagore and Gandhi—two great Indians in the twentieth century—prayed in different ways for "the magnificent harmony of all human races."

"Prisoner, tell me, who was it that bound you?"
"It was my master," said the prisoner. "I thought I could outdo everybody in the world in wealth and power, and I amassed in my own treasure house the money due to my king. When sleep overcame me I lay upon the bed that was for my lord, and on waking up I found I was a prisoner in my own treasure house."
"Prisoner, tell me, who was it that wrought this unbreakable chain?"
"It was I," said the prisoner, "who forged this chain very carefully. I thought my invincible power would hold the world captive leaving me in a freedom undisturbed. Thus night and day I worked at the chain with huge fires and cruel hard strokes. When at last the work was done and the links were complete and unbreakable, I found that it held me in its grip."

Louis Fischer contrasted the two great Indian figures in the following manner: "They were nationalists yet internationalists, sentimentally inseparable, and soulmates to the end. But they were also deeply different and waged frequent verbal battles.

"Gandhi was frugal, Tagore prodigal; Gandhi the emaciated ascetic with shaven head and face, Tagore the large, white-maned, white-bearded, rich aristocrat-intellectual with visage of classic beauty; Gandhi the rice field, Tagore the singing voice.

"Gandhi sat, so to speak, in a market place crisscrossed by tens of millions of persons with their carts, cares, wares, and thoughts, but he sat still and within him there was peace. He would have suffocated in an ivory tower or on an Olympian height, whereas Tagore said, 'If I hear a song, my sitar can catch the melody, and I can join the chorus, for I am a singer. But in the mad clamor of the crowd, my voice is lost, and I become dizzy.'

"At Shantiniketan (Tagore's home and school), Tagore's pupils sang and danced, wove garlands, and made life beautiful. When Gandhi arrived on a visit he persuaded the teachers and students to run the kitchen, collect the garbage, clean the toilets, and sweep the grounds."

Tagore observed the transformation of his school and said, "This experiment contains the key to Swaraj, or home rule."

And Gandhi had a literary lesson to teach Tagore: "True to his poetical instinct," wrote Gandhi, "the poet lives for the morrow and would have us do likewise. He presents to our admiring gaze the beautiful picture of the birds early in the morning singing hymns of praise as they soar into the sky. These birds have had their day's food and soared with rested wings in whose veins new blood had flowed during the previous night.

"I have had the pain of watching birds who for want of strength could not be coaxed even into a flutter of their wings. The human bird under the Indian sky gets up weaker than when he pretended to retire. For millions it is an eternal vigil or an eternal trance. It is an indescribably painful state which has got to be experienced to be realized.

"I have found it impossible to soothe suffering patients with a song. . . . The hungry millions ask for one poem—invigorating food. They cannot be given it. They must earn it. And they can earn it only by the sweat of their brow."

Poets speak of joyous dreams and alabaster cities where no men die or suffer pain. Gandhi thought of the same dreams and wrote, "Joy of what men call happiness may be, as it really is, a dream in a fleeting and transitory world. . . . But we cannot dismiss the suffering of our fellow creatures as unreal and thereby provide a moral alibi for ourselves. Even dreams are true while they last, and to the sufferer his suffering is a grim reality."

Nearly 500,000 Indians had fought loyally for the British during World War I, hoping that they would gain some measure of freedom when the war was done. Traditional European boundaries were changed after the war and many new democratic states emerged.

President Woodrow Wilson of the United States presented a doctrine of self-determination to the newly formed democracies. Colonial peoples all over the world were stirred by the possibility of independence. No people really wanted to be ruled by a foreign nation. Each man would like to be able to chart his own course in life.

Gandhi summed it up best when he said, "I want freedom for the full expression of my personality. I must be free to build a staircase to Sirius if I want to."

Britain, however, was not ready to yield her colonial possessions.

Gandhi and the poet Tagore became close friends, though they differed greatly in many of their ideas. Gandhi represented the mundane life of the Indian people, while Tagore was the beauty India had produced over the centuries.

Gandhiji

For security reasons, many Indians who had been agitating for home rule had been imprisoned during the war. A rigid censorship had been imposed upon the newspapers and the radio stations. Indians had been restricted in their travel. When the war was over, the Indian people expected a return of the civil liberties they had enjoyed before the war.

In 1919, however, the British government passed the Rowlatt Act, which kept India wrapped in strict, wartime controls. Loyal Indian citizens were horrified.

Gandhi and others asked the people of India to observe a nationwide *hartal* in protest. The hartal was a general strike during which time all businesses were closed and no one worked. It caused a complete cessation of commercial activity—a great inconvenience to the British.

Unfortunately, the hartal gave rise to violence and bloodshed. Indiscriminate looting, arson, and vandalism threw the cities into a state of terror. Inflamed Hindus set up blockades against trains, while others cut telegraph wires. There were repeated physical assaults against Englishmen. No one was safe in the streets.

Gandhi was mortified by the results of the hartal. He immediately began a fast of purification and urged all his satyagrahis to do the same as penance for the sins of India.

The British were quick to react. In the Punjab, a region of India, a British general set armored cars and

---

Gandhi and his wife, in 1921. At this time they lived in India, and Gandhi was editing the newspaper Young India.

soldiers with rifles upon a large group of strikers. After he ordered them to disperse and they began to run, he commanded his troops to fire upon the frightened crowd. Men, women, and children were pinned to the walls with bullets. More than 1000 were wounded, 379 killed.

Following the Punjab massacre, the determined Mahatma began to advocate complete noncooperation with the British. He urged his people to boycott British goods, British schools, and British jobs. He told Indian citizens not to pay their taxes. He also stressed nonconsumption of liquors because the British profited handsomely from the sale of alcoholic beverages.

Gandhi traveled in third-class coaches all over India to instruct the people. He gave up wearing a shirt and a cap, and wore only a loincloth, in the manner of a peasant. He preached simplicity, and told the Indians to give up their foreign clothing. When he stood before Indians who were wearing British-made clothing, he would urge them to take it all off—shirts, pants, coats, shoes—everything. They did. Then they placed all their foreign-made clothing in a huge pile and Gandhi set a match to it.

By Gandhi's example, Indian people began to spin and weave their own clothing. Gandhi himself spent more than a half hour each day spinning his own cotton. The spinning wheel became

The Punjab Massacre, in which the British killed 379 strikers and wounded 1000.

the symbol of noncooperation with the British. It was a sign of self-reliance and the hope of the poor.

Gandhi continued to insist on non-violence as the only way to practice civil disobedience, but trouble erupted, nevertheless. Savage acts were perpetrated on Hindus, Moslems, and Englishmen. Policemen were killed. India was on the verge of breaking into mass open revolt and armed rebellion against the oppressive measures of the British, but the Mahatma would not let it happen. He told Indians to keep the peace, and they listened carefully because they trusted the patient ways of this man.

There is an ancient Hindu proverb saying that the sweetness of flowers and the scent of sandalwood travel only with the wind; but the fragrance of a good man travels even against the wind and enters every place. Gandhi's acts of nonviolent civil disobedience grew like flowers of hope and determination all over India, never bending beneath the winds of British Raj and frustrating the government at every end.

Finally, in 1922, at Ahmedabad, where monkeys run freely in the streets and are too numerous to cage, the British government in India took Gandhi to trial. He was charged with "bringing or attempting to bring into hatred or contempt or exciting or attempting to excite disaffection towards His Majesty's Government."

The heart of India lay open at the Great Trial. The Mahatma's future was at stake. Was not the future of India also at stake? Many Indian patriots had already been found guilty of this same act, and had been jailed.

Gandhi pleaded guilty to all charges. The prosecution, not satisfied with Gandhi's plea, went on to try to prove that Gandhi's whole life was nothing but the uncompromising record of a rebel. Gandhi was depicted as an ungrateful wretch who led boycotts, strikes, burned British clothing in the streets, incited people to agitation, and wrote seditious articles.

The British judge, C. N. Broomsfield, listened with detachment. He knew that even as India's spiritual leader was being tried for various acts against the British policy in India, that the British Raj itself was on trial.

Eventually it was Gandhi's turn to defend himself. He agreed to all the charges. But he also explained how, for most of his life, he had been a loyal defender of the British Empire. He recalled how he had served the British during the Boer War and again during World War I.

Then, as he stood before the judge's bench, the small, bespectacled man read a prepared statement in his usual high-pitched, modest, and singsong voice: "If one has no affection for a person or a system, one should be free to give the fullest expression to his disaffection, so long as he does not contemplate, promote or incite to violence."

Gandhi looked at Judge Broomsfield in a friendly way and continued: "I hold it to be a virtue to be disaffected towards a government which in its totality has done more harm to India than any previous system. India is less manly under the British rule than she ever was before."

With utmost confidence, Gandhi said, "I am here, therefore, to invite and submit cheerfully to the highest penalty that can be inflicted upon me for what in law is a deliberate crime and what appears to me to be the highest duty of a citizen."

With a sense of deep humiliation, Gandhi twisted the last bit of irony from the trial: "The only course open to you, the judge, is either to resign your post and thus dissociate yourself from evil, if you feel that the law you are called upon to administer is an evil and thus in reality I am innocent; or to inflict on me the severest penalty if you believe that the system and the law you are assisting to administer are good for the people of this country and that my activity is therefore injurious to the public weal."

Then the little man, whose life was the hope of all India, sat down.

Judge Broomsfield handed down his decision reluctantly. "The law is no respecter of persons," said the judge. "Nevertheless, it will be impossible to ignore the fact that you are in a different category from any person I have ever tried or am likely to have to try. It would be impossible to ignore the fact that, in the eyes of millions of your countrymen, you are a great patriot and a great leader. Even those who differ from you in politics look upon you as a man of high ideals and of noble and of even saintly life.

"There are probably few people in India who do not sincerely regret that you should have made it impossible for any government to leave you at liberty. But it is so."

The judge sentenced Gandhi to six years in prison and added with typical British fairness, "If the course of events in India should make it possible for the Government to reduce the period and release you, no one will be better pleased than I."

Gandhi's reply was equally amiable: "So far as the whole proceedings are concerned, I must say that I could not have expected greater courtesy."

Spectators fell before his feet and wept as he was led away, but Gandhi went to jail in good spirits. He had knowingly broken the law, and he was willing to accept the punishment. His example encouraged millions of others to do the same. No government can exist without the cooperation of those

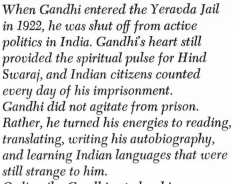

When Gandhi entered the Yeravda Jail in 1922, he was shut off from active politics in India. Gandhi's heart still provided the spiritual pulse for Hind Swaraj, and Indian citizens counted every day of his imprisonment.

Gandhi did not agitate from prison. Rather, he turned his energies to reading, translating, writing his autobiography, and learning Indian languages that were still strange to him.

Ordinarily, Gandhi acted as his own doctor whenever he or anyone else got sick. He advocated a light diet, including only certain foods, as the proper way to heal the sick. He believed in using mud packs, water baths, and massages in order to hold down his temperature or check his frequent attacks of high blood pressure.

In 1924, Gandhi suffered an attack of acute appendicitis. Against appendicitis, his home remedies could do nothing. British officials immediately transferred him from prison to a small hospital at Poona. The British were afraid that Gandhi might die and that his death would cause a civil war in India.

A British surgeon recommended an immediate operation. Gandhi agreed to it and told the doctor, "I am your prisoner. I cannot claim any privilege that cannot be claimed by others."

He even signed a document saying that the operation was done with his own consent, so that there would be no misunderstandings on the part of edgy Indian politicians if anything went wrong.

The operation began late in the evening. Overhead a thunderstorm was raging. The storm cut the electricity in the small operating room. Nurses held flashlights while the doctor worked laboriously over the body of the Mahatma, who had been given chloroform. Then the batteries burned out as Gandhi's life was in the balance. For the remainder of the operation, a nurse held a hurricane lantern over the operating table. The dim, flickering light cast ominous shadows on the walls.

The operation was successful, but infectious complications later led to Gandhi's early release from prison. The skills of a British doctor probably saved the life of the man who would eventually slay the British Lion in India.

people it rules, and British colonialism in India was beginning to deteriorate.

Gandhi worked hard in jail. He read, he wrote, he thought about the problems of India, and he translated poetry. He refused to be an idle man. In 1924, he was stricken by an attack of acute appendicitis. A British surgeon operated on him, but the Mahatma was slow in healing. Officials of the British government thought it a wise gesture to release him. Within two months, Gandhi was back at work editing *Young India*, a weekly newspaper he had founded in 1919.

When his words failed, Gandhi would turn to the fast as the means of communicating deeply with his people. Fasting was a religious gesture that had profound significance for India. Masses of people were deeply moved by the little man who sat cross-legged, swaying back and forth with his palms together in the Hindu blessing and with a benign smile on his face. He said nothing, for all India knew what his fasts meant—peace in India.

Over the centuries, many Hindus had converted to Islam. Many had married Moslem girls. In certain areas, Moslems worshiped in Hindu temples. In most of India's 700,000 villages, Hindus and Moslems got along very peacefully. But in the growing industrial cities, where the extremes of wealth and poverty were much more acute and people lived in closer economic competition, the religious differences created problems. Cruelhearted Moslems thought little of butchering the Hindu sacred cows, and the Hindus insulted Moslems by singing in front of their mosques during services. City politicians, in order to gain power, magnified these religious differences and set man against man.

In 1924, Gandhiji, as many called him (the "ji" on the end of a Hindu

Gandhi answering mail in his study. As his fame spread throughout India and the world, he found himself an extremely busy man, but he never neglected his goal of peace for India.

name was an expression of affection), began a twenty-one-day fast in the house of a Moslem as a demonstration of religious brotherhood. He was attended by two Moslem doctors in order to show the Hindus that he trusted Moslems. During this fast he wrote articles preaching tolerance of all religions. Upon breaking the fast, he asked that his friends recite the opening verses of the Koran (the Moslem bible), sing a Christian hymn, and then sing a Hindu hymn. This was Gandhiji's way of calling forth the cause of brotherhood. It was Gandhiji's mission to achieve harmonious relations between his Hindu and Moslem brothers. It would also become his greatest failure.

Because of his nonviolent ways and his devotion to religious purpose, the unwashed masses of India began to think of Gandhi as a great holy man. The public began to make an idol of the Mahatma. Believers crowded him wherever he went. It disturbed him to see people wearing his picture around their necks and he asked them not to do it. He was not a god and he knew it. He was only trying to be as near to holiness as he could be.

"They will not leave me alone even when I am taking my bath," he wrote. His feet and legs were covered with scratches left by men, women, and children who fell before him and reached out for him, hoping that some of his godliness would rub off on them.

All that glory and adoration meant nothing to Gandhi. It did not fill the bellies of the hungry; it did not lift the burdens of the poor; it did not free the spirit of India from the shackles of British Raj. The *Gita* taught that he who eats without labor eats sin and is a thief. Gandhi's goal was to teach India the dignity of labor so that each man could raise himself up by the skills of his own hands.

Gandhi traveled all over India teaching everyone to make homespun cotton —*khadi*—by means of home spinning wheels. He told them to use khadi for clothing, shawls, towels, and bed sheets. The whole of India from sea to sea was turning white with homespun cotton.

Wherever he went he was able to collect money in order to buy spinning wheels for peasants who could not afford them. He was also able to organize the training of weavers, who in turn taught their skills to the poor and the ignorant.

There was growing resistance to his cause, however. Younger politicians were attaining status; Jawaharlal Nehru was one of these brilliant men. He believed in Gandhi and a free India but objected to Gandhi's simple means. Nehru felt that India must recognize the age of machines and industrialization. He said that efficient industrial organization could do much more than spinning wheels in the home to better the living conditions of the impoverished masses of India.

But Gandhi distrusted machines. He had seen the dismal factory areas of London and the working and living conditions of the laborers who slaved four-

An industrial workers' ghetto of the type found in Bombay and Calcutta. Gandhi distrusted machinery and industrialization because he felt men would be demoralized and dignity would be removed from human labor.

teen hours a day in the English factories. He had seen the slums and factory ghettos of Bombay and Calcutta feed filth and crime into the already congested cities. He feared that machines would displace the value and dignity of human labor and thus demoralize human beings.

"Machinery merely helps a few to ride on the backs of millions," observed Gandhi. Machinery concentrated the tools of production in the hands of a few industrialists who tended to monopolize labor and control the distribution of all goods.

Gandhi was also apprehensive about the possibility of mass unemployment as machines took work away from the people. Would it increase India's tendency toward "grinding pauperism?" Furthermore, who stood to gain more by the use of machines—the Indians or the British?

Yes, Gandhi admitted that the spinning wheel and the sewing machine were machines. But at least the person working with these machines could enjoy the fruits of his own labor. He was not dependent on industrialists for his needs.

Gandhi envisioned India as an economic network of self-reliant, self-governing villages that traded with each other for their basic needs. He believed that people were happier when they lived a simple village existence. In the city, people were too crowded, too competitive, and too criminal. The urban mass loomed as a threat to humanity.

There was a time in 1930 when Gandhi
and his followers were gathered in a
camp that lay at Karadi, a small hamlet
in the Mahatma's home state of
Gujarat. Gandhi as usual was at his
hut making khadi on his spinning wheel,
called a charkha.
Gandhi's hut was made of mud walls
and covered with a thatched roof of
grass. It was his desire to share the
frugal existence of the poorest peasant.
All of a sudden singing was heard.
A group of villagers were marching in
a procession around the campsite.
Women singing hymns were in front,
and men followed carrying fruit, flowers,
and bags of money. After they circled
the campsite, the men came forward and
placed their gifts at Gandhi's feet as if
he were an image of the great Buddha.
Gandhi was markedly puzzled by the
demonstration and asked the village
headman what the offerings meant.
The headman faltered, but then told
Gandhi the following story: His village
possessed a well that had not yielded
water for many years.
One day recently, Gandhi had walked
through their village; the feet of the
Mahatma had touched their soil.
On that same day water came rising
from the well that had been dry for
so many years.
"We have come to worship you," said
the headman, "for you must be an
incarnation of the great God Rama."
At first Gandhi was visibly shaken.
He did not like to be called God.
But soon he mellowed and related the
following allegory to the villagers as
he stopped to mend a piece of thread:
"Suppose what you say has happened.
Surely it is a coincidence. Consider the
case of the crow who comes to sit on
an old palm tree at the very moment
that tree is falling to the ground. Do you
think it was the weight of the crow that
caused the tree's uprooting?"
"It is foolish and unbecoming of you
to worship me," admonished Gandhi
firmly. "I have no more influence with
God than you have."
Gandhi then asked the villagers to
return to their homes and not waste time
speculating about his divinity. He urged
them to turn their time and energy to
the important task of helping India
gain independence from the British rule.

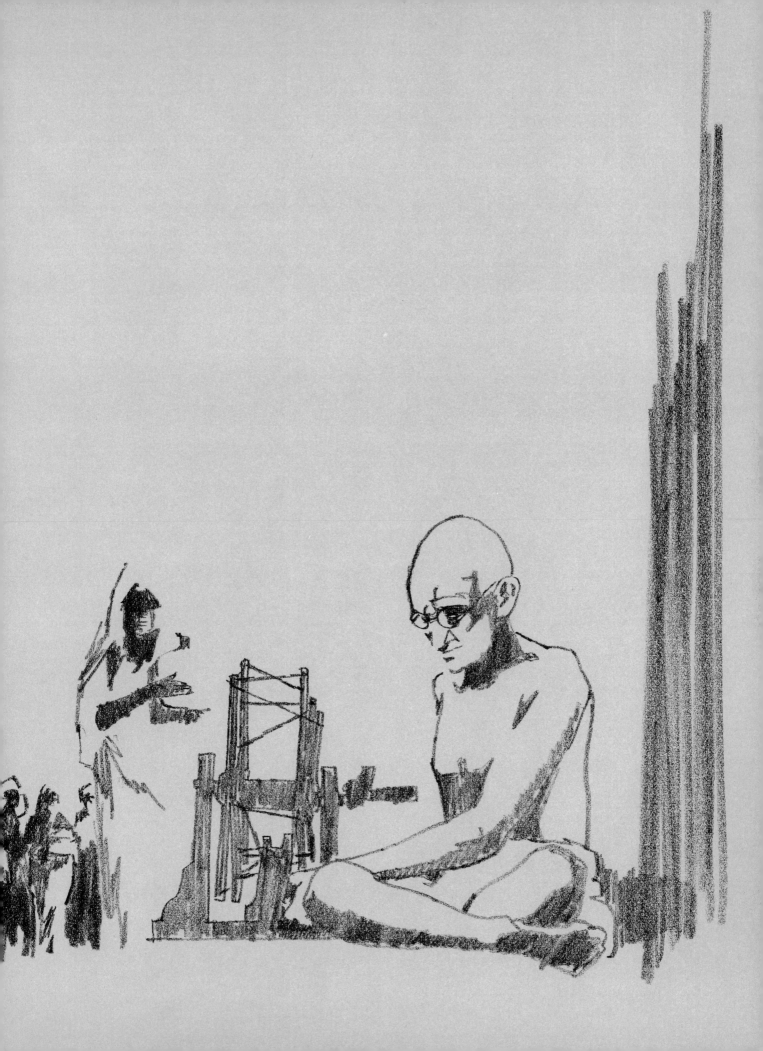

The Salt Laws

Repeated attempts had been made by Gandhi and members of the Indian Congress Party to work out a gentleman's agreement for equal partnership in the British Empire. English statesmen would have no part of it. In 1930, therefore, Gandhi finally decided to begin engaging in civil disobedience with complete independence for India as his goal. He waited for the most propitious moment to signal his intentions to the British.

The time had come. Gandhi sent a letter to the British viceroy of India, Lord Irwin, informing him of his plans to break the salt laws.

"Dear Friend," wrote Gandhi, "Before embarking on Civil Disobedience and taking the risk I have dreaded to take all these years, I would fain approach you to find a way out. . . . I cannot intentionally hurt anything that lives, much less human beings, even though they may do the greatest wrong to me and mine. . . . Whilst, therefore, I hold the British rule to be a curse, I do not intend harm to a single Englishman or to prevent any legitimate interest he may have in India. . . .

"And why do I regard the English rule as a curse? It has impoverished the dumb millions by a system of progressive exploitation and a ruinous expensive military and civil administration which the country can never afford.

"It has reduced us politically to serfdom. It has sapped the foundations of our culture. . . . I fear . . . there has never been any intention of granting . . . dominion Status to India in the immediate future. . . ."

Thus Gandhi began his historic march to the sea to take a pinch of salt. Within a month, he was arrested and put in jail without trial. He went to prison in good spirits.

The world became very conscious of Gandhi's plight in India, and England was deluged with requests for the Mahatma's release. Acts of civil disobedience continued and were seriously encumbering the British administration. Sixty thousand Indians were placed in jails. The government's revenue dropped sharply. The Salt March proved to England that she could not govern India against the will of its people.

Gandhi spinning "the long threads of India's destiny" while being interviewed by an American newsman, in 1931.

Early the next year, the British viceroy buckled to world pressures and released Gandhi, Nehru, and other political leaders. Lord Irwin invited Gandhi for a political discussion. After several talks, the two leaders reached an agreement. All political prisoners were released. In return, civil disobedience was stopped. Salt manufacture was permitted on the seacoast, and representatives of the Indian Congress Party would go to London to air their grievances.

There was a man in London who had once served as a British soldier in India. He was very much opposed to Indian independence. His name was Winston Churchill and he was a statesman of the first rank.

Churchill knew that England could not afford to lose her colonial possessions without suffering damage and shrinkage to the Empire. He presented his case against Gandhi to the British people with splendid eloquence and bitter invective: "I am against this surrender to Gandhi. I am against these conversations and agreements between Lord Irwin and Mr. Gandhi. Gandhi stands for the expulsion of Britain from India. Gandhi stands for the permanent exclusion of British trade from India. . . . It is alarming and also nauseating to see Mr. Gandhi, a seditious Middle Temple Lawyer, now posing as a fakir, striding half-naked up the steps of the viceregal palace to parley on equal terms with the representative of the King-Emperor. . . . You will never be able to come to terms with Gandhi."

Shortly after reaching the compromise agreement with Irwin, Gandhi sailed for England. It was the summer of 1931. Wearing his usual loincloth, sandals, and shawl, he carried the case of India's plea for independence to many important people. He visited with old friends and even had tea with King George and Queen Mary at Buckingham Palace. Only Winston Churchill refused to see him.

The little "half-naked fakir" made speeches all over England. He told the British people that he wanted India to be an equal partner with Britain, sharing her joys and sorrows, and an equal partner with Britain's dominions. He spoke of "voluntary interdependence" and said that he did not want India to be isolated from England.

Wherever he went, he was accompanied by two burly Scotland Yard detectives assigned to him for his protection. They got along so well with Gandhiji that he practically considered them members of his family. All over England he spread goodwill and received tremendous support from the common people.

But England would not release her grip on India, and Gandhi had to go home empty-handed.

Immediately on his return to India, he was arrested and jailed without trial. A new government had come to power in England and the new viceroy of India wanted to take no chances with the Indian leaders who espoused independence.

Once again the Mahatma was a model prisoner, gaining the affections of his fellow inmates as well as his jailers. He spent his hours thinking about India's future, reading and writing.

Gandhi attending a conference in London, on September 14, 1931. He spent the summer of 1931 trying to convince the English to give India her independence, but was unsuccessful in his efforts.

The drastic problems of India's sixty million Untouchables began to hammer away at the Mahatma's mind. How could they be helped? How could they be uplifted?

The Untouchables had been segregated from the rest of Hindu caste society by centuries of prejudice. They did all the dirtiest jobs and lived in secluded ghettos. It was an unpardonable sin if their shadow crossed the shadow of a higher-caste Hindu. Most caste Hindus called them "pariahs," which is the same name given to mongrel dogs that roamed unwanted in the streets.

Gandhi wanted to raise their standard of living and make them acceptable to the other Hindu castes. He called them *Harijans*, meaning children of God. He even changed the name of his newspaper from *Young India* to *Harijan*.

England was on the verge of creating a separate electoral process for the Untouchables when Gandhi put his foot down. He knew that it was essential for the Untouchables to vote as part of the general Hindu population or they would be crushed forever by the greater number of prejudiced, caste Hindus.

While still in prison he decided to begin a fast until death. His aim was to unite Untouchables with other members of the Hindu society—or else perish. Political leaders tried to divert him.

When Tagore heard that Gandhi was willing to sacrifice his life in order to save the soul of India—one people, one land—he wrote, "A shadow is darkening today over India like a shadow cast by an eclipsed sun. . . . No civilized society

A bomb explodes near Gandhi while he is praying. Many assassination attempts were made on Gandhi's life, but he never bothered about them because he did not fear death.

72

can thrive upon victims whose humanity has been permanently mutilated."

Gandhi's fast was aimed at reforming great moral weakness. The news broke quickly across India. The people asked, "Why is the Mahatma fasting?"

The answer was, "Because we Hindus close our temples to Untouchables and treat them badly."

India's conscience was stirred when people heard that the fast was taking its toll on the sixty-three-year-old man. While the fast was still going on, Hindu leaders met with leaders of the Untouchables to see what could be done. They worked quickly to achieve a joint electorate, and the Hindus reserved seats in the legislature for the Harijans, who in turn would democratically elect members to fill these seats.

The major result of this fast was the Yeravda Pact of 1932, named after the prison which had housed Gandhi for so many months. The pact was immediately accepted by India and England, and Gandhi broke the fast that had lasted six days. From that day forward, no human being could be considered an Untouchable by birth according to the law.

Gandhi's victory did not leave him without enemies. Certain caste Hindus believed that it was wrong to meddle with the religious traditions of centuries, and they began to look upon the Mahatma with a burning hatred. The man who was a friend to all religions and all peoples of the world was gaining enemies at home among his own Hindu brothers.

Before he could fast again, he was released unconditionally from prison.

During the years 1934-1939, Gandhiji devoted his life to social betterment. He felt that politics was better left to younger men. He traveled from village to village promoting spinning, education, proper diet, and sanitation; and he encouraged the spread of Hindi and Hindustani as the national language. Several attempts were made on his life, but he brushed them off with hardly any concern. He simply did not fear death, nor did he resent those who disagreed with his policies.

The Mahatma was always happy to receive visitors and frequently gave interviews to newsmen and writers. He even agreed to speak to the American people on a radio broadcast. Some people were curious about his beliefs and others just wanted to be near him. He was warmhearted and joked with anyone he considered a friend, and it seemed that anyone who ever met him instantly became his friend. He felt love for all human beings.

In the late 1930's, Gandhi tried to seclude himself at a hermitage called Sevagram near Wardha in the central provinces of India. There he lived with his wife and a small community of disciples in mud huts with palm leaf mats on the earthen floors. Anyone visiting him had to stand or sit cross-legged on the floor.

Sevagram was the refuge for a strange group of human beings who all shared in the household chores such as cooking, cleaning, and washing. They

even raised their own food and cultured their own dairy products.

Among them were a Jewish refugee from Germany who was under the influence of an Indian wise man; a Sanskrit scholar who had contracted leprosy and lived in the hut next to Gandhi's where he received daily attention from the Mahatma; a hardworking Japanese monk who walked around the campsite beating a drum and chanting Buddhist prayers, and whom certain critics believed was a spy for Japan; a Hindu princess who had renounced her wealth and worldly possessions; and a religious man who did not believe in work in any form and liked to walk barefooted and naked through the forests fearing neither snakes nor scorpions. The religious man had come to Sevagram without a stitch of clothing, wearing nothing but a copper ring sewn through his lips. Gandhi convinced him to wear a loincloth, and the man who despised work began religiously to spend seventeen hours a day at the spinning wheel. They seemed like a collection of misfits, but Gandhi loved them all.

When important people like Nehru or the Aga Khan came to see Gandhi about affairs of state, he received them while lying on the floor with mudpacks on his head and abdomen to protect himself from high blood pressure and the heat of the day. At times he would even keep them waiting while he spent hours analyzing the bad dreams of children or discussing the proper thickness of soup in the community kitchen.

Many people came to Gandhi to be healed from some imaginary or real sickness. The Mahatma began to refer to Sevagram as "a home for invalids and lunatics."

His day was very exacting in terms of time. He arose precisely at 3:00 A.M., before the birds began chirping. He occupied himself with reading and writing before the others awoke. Then he washed himself carefully and cleaned his teeth. After morning prayers, he ate a meager breakfast of fruits and toast.

Between 4:00 and 5:00 A.M., he took his morning walk. This was the time of the day he allotted to interviews with foreign newsmen; they had to jog after him if they were interested. The remainder of the morning was devoted to helping the sick.

At 11:00 A.M., all patients were fed in Gandhi's hut according to his strict instructions on diet. After lunch, he read through his vast volume of mail as well as the daily newspapers. Then he took a nap.

In the afternoon, he received that endless line of Indian people wanting to interview him on some problem or another. In the late afternoon, he devoted one hour to spinning.

Dinner was at 5:00 P.M. His final meal consisted of dates, nuts, and curd. After dinner, he took his usual evening walk while children followed and assailed him with questions. It pleased Gandhi to be able to joke with the children.

Evening prayers were held for all. Gandhi sat in the middle of the group while verses about the ideal man were read from the *Bhagavad Gita*. Each night Gandhi delivered a short sermon dealing with the various illnesses, the

Gandhi converses with Rabindranath Tagore. The two men, though good friends, had very different views on India; Gandhi saw it as a country of poor, starving masses who must be uplifted, while Tagore saw India as "the eternal ragpicker at other people's dustbins."

day's mistakes of his wife, or India's struggle against the British Raj.

When night fell, Gandhi lay on a cot in the open air or on the veranda of his hut. He spent several moments observing the vast expanse of stars, the myriad stellar mysteries, and the infinite realm of space as he fell asleep listening to the music of the spheres.

Such was a typical day in Gandhi's life in the late 1930's.

An American minister once asked Gandhi what caused him the most concern and Gandhi replied, "The hardness of heart of the educated."

Gandhi's religious beliefs had universal appeal. He felt that the teachings of religion should concentrate on ethics and human conduct by helping to make men and women better men and women. He said, "All religions are almost as dear to me as my own Hinduism, in as much as all human beings should be as dear to one as one's own close relatives."

His definition of God was related to all human experience in the real world, not to an abstract deity who existed in a faraway heavenly paradise where no human being ever set foot.

Gandhi wrote: "God is that indefinable something which we all feel but which we do not know. To me God is Truth and Love, God is ethics and morality. God is fearlessness. God is the source of light and life and yet He is above and beyond all these. God is conscience. He is even the atheism of the atheist. He transcends speech and reason. He is a personal God to those who need His Touch. He is the purest essence. He simply is to those who have faith. He is long suffering. He is patient but He is also terrible. He is the greatest democrat the world knows, for He leaves us unfettered to make our own choice between evil and good. He is the greatest tyrant ever known for He often dashes the cup from our lips and under cover of free will leaves us a margin so wholly inadequate as to provide only mirth for himself at our expense. Therefore, it is that Hinduism calls all this sport—*Lila*, or calls it an illusion—*Maya*."

Gandhi enjoys a chuckle with the Hindu leader Jawaharlal Nehru at opening day of the All India Congress Committee, July 6, 1946. Above, Gandhi relaxes in a cot on his veranda.

Hind Swaraj

In 1939, Europe was once again embroiled in a full-scale war. The Nazi Party had risen to power in Germany and the Fascists gained power in Italy. Adolf Hitler, dictator of Germany, with token support from Benito Mussolini, the Italian dictator, set forth to conquer France, England, and Russia. These two men wanted to unify Europe into one economic bloc. They were aided by the imperial forces in Japan who assaulted China, Burma, and some Pacific island groups, eventually attacking the United States at Pearl Harbor, in Hawaii.

England threw India into the conflagration of World War II without consulting the Indian people. Gandhi, Nehru, and the Indian Congress Party were irritated. They began stirring up acts of civil disobedience. They saw the issue of India's cooperation during World War II as a lever for independence, and they wanted a guarantee from England before giving full support to the war effort.

Gandhi said, "War is wrong, war is an unmitigated evil." But he did not want India scorched by Japan, who was already ravaging in Burma and pressing toward the borders of India. He was willing to permit English and American troops to use India as a base of operations. Germany, Italy, and Japan were aggressor nations and had to be stopped.

Gandhi wrote to President Franklin D. Roosevelt, who championed Gandhi's cause. Roosevelt in turn put pressure on Prime Minister Winston Churchill. Most Americans were fully in support of Gandhi's quest for a free India and this embarrassed their British allies. Churchill refused to budge. He said,

This group of Indians is lying in front of a train, protesting the lack of diplomacy on the part of the British in ruling India. Gandhi and his followers continued to use civil disobedience as a tactic to disrupt British rule.

"I have not become the King's First Minister in order to preside at the liquidation of the British Empire."

Owing to the pressing needs of wartime, England had dispensed with diplomacy. This made it increasingly hard to rule India. Violence erupted. Disenchanted Indians struck everywhere, setting government buildings on fire and tore up railroad ties. They cut down telegraph wires and congested traffic. A political underground developed and "Quit India" campaigns pestered the British Raj.

England wasted no time putting political agitators in jail. Gandhi was one of the first; he and his wife were imprisoned in the palace of the Aga Khan. It was here that Kasturbai died in Gandhi's arms, in 1944. She was seventy-four years old and had been the Mahatma's faithful wife for sixty-one years. After her death, Gandhi's health began to decline and he was released from imprisonment.

For the most part, India did not seriously want to embarrass the British war efforts. More than one million Indian soldiers—Hindus, Moslems, and Sikhs—served the British and her allies bravely in North Africa, in Italy, in the eastern Mediterranean, and on the borders of India.

General Dwight D. Eisenhower led the final push against the Germans from the west at Normandy, and the Russians closed in from the east. The "invincible" powers of Germany were pinched into unconditional surrender. General Douglas MacArthur controlled the Pacific and the United States dropped two atomic bombs which put an end to the hostilities in Japan.

England had been battered too badly at home to continue to rule her colonies effectively. The government at home changed from Conservative to Labour hands. Churchill was out as prime minister as the Labour Party took charge. The new leaders were only too happy to relinquish England's two-century hold on India, to the relief of the Indian people.

Gandhi's Final Fast

Now that the Indian goals had been accomplished, the problem that faced the British in India was how to effect the transfer of power. There was also the problem of the vast rift between Hindus and Moslems.

India's long, hard struggle was seemingly over with the immediate promise of independence. But the bloodiest battle was yet to be fought. Who would protect Hindus from Moslems when the British troops were removed? Who would protect Moslems from Hindus? The old religious hatreds split the country into two political factions. Who would rule when the British were gone?

Religious fervor now began to burn across the face of the land. The Moslems, who were only a quarter of the population of all India, feared that the Hindu majority would crush them politically.

Under the leadership of Mohammed Ali Jinnah, Moslems campaigned for the separate and independent state of Pakistan—the Land of the Pure. Since Moslems were in the majority in northwest and northeast India, they wanted those sections of land set off as separate Moslem states. They were willing to leave the remainder of India to the Hindus and the Sikhs, tall bearded warriors who, as a reform movement, had founded a casteless society, breaking off from traditional Hindu customs.

Gandhi insisted on a united India with Moslems and Hindus living in harmony. He felt that the two cultures had been intertwined for too many centuries to be ripped apart at this time. He underestimated the divisive forces of the old religious hatreds.

Moslem leader Mohammed Ali Jinnah pointed out the critical differences: "How can you even dream of Hindu-Moselm unity? Everything pulls us apart: We have no intermarriages. We have not the same calendar. The Moslems believe in a single god, and the Hindus are idolatrous. Like the Christians, the Moslems believe in an equalitarian society, whereas the Hindus maintain the iniquitous system of castes and leave heartlessly fifty million Untouchables to their tragic fate, at the bottom of the social ladder. The Hindus worship animals. They consider cows sacred. We, the Moslems, think it is

British troops leave India after independence is granted.

nonsense. We want to kill the cows. We want to eat them. Another thing: No Hindu will even take food from a Moslem. No orthodox Hindu will even touch Hindu food if the shadow of a Moslem or the shadow of a Hindu of a lower caste has polluted the bowl."

It seemed that the only practical step was to partition parts of India and create the separate states of West Pakistan and East Pakistan. Almost all Hindu and Moslem leaders agreed to this—except Gandhi. England helped in setting the boundaries.

What followed independence and the partition of Pakistan was one of the cruelest bloodbaths of modern history. Vast migrations cut India into shreds. Moslems carried whatever they owned to their new states. Hindus living in the northwest and northeast fled their homes to escape the scourge of the oncoming Moslems.

Civil war broke out and Moslems and Hindus cut each other down in the streets indiscriminately. Fanatics attacked each other in their homes. The cry "Blood for Blood" spread through the cities. Hysterical mobs ruled the day and nearly a half-million people were killed. What was worse, fifteen million people were left as homeless refugees.

Gandhi could do nothing except try to keep the peace. Nearly in despair he said, "I have not convinced India. There is violence all around us. I am a spent bullet."

Wherever there was trouble—in Calcutta, Bombay, and New Delhi—Gandhi rushed there to pacify the crowds. He was nearly overcome by what he called, "a sickening feeling at the mass madness that can turn man into less than a brute."

Many Moslems had good homes and businesses in Indian cities and they were not about to leave them. One of the worst incidents happened at a famous Moslem school in a village near New Delhi.

According to Louis Fischer, "The school found itself engulfed in a sea of angry Sikh and Hindu refugees and neighborhood peasants to whom everything Islamic, whether man or edifice, was hateful. At night the students and teachers stood guard, expecting an

Civil war in India over the partitioning of Pakistan. The hatred between Moslems and Hindus reached a violent peak at this time.

82

assault hourly. In a circle around them they could see Moslem villages in flames and Moslem homes put to the torch.

"Nearby flows the Jumna. Night after night they could hear howling Moslems jump into the river to escape their pursuers, and then the pursuers would jump in after them, and there were scuffles and splashes and the victim would be held down until he drowned or gave one last anguished screech as the knife descended on his bare throat."

At great personal danger, Jawaharlal Nehru, the prime minister of the New Republic of India, and the indefatigable Mr. Gandhi rushed to the aid of the school. Their presence managed to bring peace to the community.

Gandhi looked upon the street violence of Delhi with tears in his eyes. He could hardly believe what he saw. In order to bring peace to Delhi, he decided to fast until death. "Death for me," he said, "would be a glorious deliverance rather than I should be a helpless witness to the destruction of India, Hinduism, Sikhism, and Islam."

On January 13, 1948, at the age of seventy-eight, the Mahatma began his last fast. India was shocked. Thousands walked by his porch, where the Mahatma lay crouched with his knees tucked into his stomach and his fists into his chest. They wept for their holy man. Nobody wanted Bapu to die.

While Gandhi's heartbeat was failing, the new government of India released 180 million dollars in rupees to the government of Pakistan, which was her share of the assets of pre-partition India.

Finally, on January 18, when several leaders came to Gandhi and pledged harmony for all religious people as well as help for all the political refugees, Gandhi broke his fast by taking a glass of fruit juice. Peace had been restored to Delhi. For several days afterward,

Gandhi was so weak that he had to be carried to the prayer grounds.

Certain Hindus, however, still felt very bitter toward Gandhi. They thought he was responsible for giving away too much of India to the Moslems. They felt he was betraying his caste. These selfish men taught others to hate the Mahatma. A bomb was thrown from the garden wall while Gandhi and others were at prayers. Fortunately, Gandhi escaped injury and hardly allowed his prayers to be disturbed.

Gandhi had wanted to live to be 125 years old. With all the interreligious warfare between Hindus, Moslems, and Sikhs, though, he had become disillusioned. Toward the end, he spoke of his own death several times. "I do not want to die . . . of creeping paralysis of my faculties—a defeated man. An assassin's bullet may put an end to my life. I would welcome it."

On the fateful evening of Friday, January 30, 1948, the Mahatma met his end. He had eaten dinner and was on his way to evening prayers where a congregation of five hundred persons was waiting, including a man by the name of Godse.

Godse was a Hindu of the Brahman caste and the editor of a newspaper. He had been incensed by the success of Gandhi's recent fast, and decided to put an end to the authority which the Mahatma commanded.

Godse pushed his way through the crowd and fell on his knees before the Mahatma in a gesture of reverence. He pulled a small pistol from his pocket and fired three shots at Gandhi.

As he fell, Gandhi was heard to murmur, "Oh Ram, Oh Ram," for he had been taught as a child to call the name of his god whenever he was in trouble.

His limp body crumbled to the earth, his leather sandals slipped from his feet, his glasses lay in the dust.

The Mahatma was dead.

Gandhi at the microphone speaking to his people in the cause of Indian peace.

According to Hindu custom, Gandhi's body was cremated the next day. A million and a half people of all faiths marched in the funeral procession to the banks of the Jumna River, the site of the pyre, where another million people were waiting.

White was seen everywhere, the color of homespun khadi. People were dressed in white saris and suits, white caps and turbans. They stood in the river and climbed into the trees in order to get a better view. Practically everyone was chanting—Mahatma Gandhi Ki Jai! Mahatma Gandhi Ki Jai! Long live Mahatma Gandhi! Victory to Mahatma Gandhi!

Gandhi's body was carefully placed on the top of a neat pile of sandalwood logs that had been sprinkled with incense. His head was to the north, his feet to the south. In the same manner, Buddha had met his end.

Gandhi's third son, Ramdas, set the fire. As the logs burst into flames, a great groan went up from the huge gathering of people. Tears were in everyone's eyes.

The pyre burned for fourteen hours. Gandhi's ashes were placed in a homespun cotton bag and kept with the family for the customary thirteen days. Then the ashes were immersed in the seven sacred rivers of India. Thus Mahatma's last remains coursed an eternal path through the holy veins of his motherland.

India's Great Soul was freed from the cycles of life and death.

On January 31, 1948, the day of Gandhi's funeral in New Delhi, crowds try to surge forward to the funeral pyre but are held back by the authorities.

India goes on. The acrid smoke from small dung fires can be seen rising throughout the cities in curls of yellowish haze. Water buffalo roam the streets. Hindus of higher castes still fear pollution by the shadows of the lower castes. New bridges, dams, and factories are being built, but the slow, ancient pace of India tends to hold back the progress of the new age.

There is need for land reform. Vinoba Bhave, a disciple of Gandhi, walks from village to village asking the rich to donate gifts of land to the poor. They call him the Walking Saint. Because of Bhave and the memory of Gandhi, the wealthy landowners have given over four million acres of tillable land to the poor so that they might own and work their own farms.

After India's independence, even Winston Churchill had a change of heart. He told the British people: "Our imperial mission in India is at an end — we must recognize that. Some day justice will be done by world opinion to our record there, but the chapter is closed . . . we must look forward. It is our duty, whatever part we have taken in the past, to hope and pray for the well-being and happiness of all the peoples of India . . . we must wish them all well and do what we can to help them on their road. Sorrow may lie in our hearts but bitterness and malice must be purged from them, and in our future more remote relations with India we must rise above all prejudice and partiality and not allow our vision to be clouded by memories of glories that are gone forever."

To the western world Gandhi was somewhat of an enigma. He held no real power by means of military strength or political office, nor did he have the advantage of great wealth. Yet his authority in India and the world was far-reaching. He held up the banner of

Where the mind is without fear
and the head is held high;
Where knowledge is free;
Where the world has not been broken up
into fragments by narrow domestic walls;
Where words come out from the depths of truth;
Where tireless striving stretches its arms
towards perfection;
Where the clear stream of reason has not lost its way
into the dreary desert sand of dead habit;
Where the mind is led forward by thee
into ever-widening thought and action—
Into that heaven of freedom, my Father,
let my country awake.

satyagraha and marched with his "soldiers of peace" to realize a free India. He was as much a result of India's history as he was an architect of her future.

Gandhi devoted his life to the service of humanity. His mission served not only the masses of India but also the entire family of man. He conceived of all the peoples and all the nations of the world as one human family with an infinite multiplicity of human wants.

Gandhi's place in history resulted from human necessity. "If we are to make progress," he said, "we must not repeat history but make new history. We must add to the inheritance left by our ancestors." Gandhi worked patiently not just for the good of the majority, but for the greater good of all. He was one of the few men who was active in political life yet did not betray his religious nature. Nor did he betray his fellow man. He made no false promises and spoke no false words. His creed was truth in all things.

One of his great admirers was Albert Einstein, the scientist dedicated to peace. Einstein considered Gandhi's views the most enlightened of any political figure at any time.

Gandhi's influence on one American citizen was most profound. Dr. Martin Luther King, Jr., had witnessed what Gandhi achieved in India and became an advocate of nonviolent resistance in the United States. He led peace marches and demonstrated for fair laws. He wanted fair treatment for Negroes. He wanted to root out the Negro ghettos that fed depraved human suffering in the very heart of wealthy America. Like Gandhi, King was assassinated for trying to change ugly social conditions. Like Gandhi's life, Dr. King's life also shines as a beacon of hope for the despised poor and the underprivileged.

What has happened to India since the death of her Mahatma? In the wake of World War II, world power became polarized between the two great nuclear nations—the U.S.S.R. and the United States—with their respective allies. The world stands today thus divided in a state of relatively peaceful coexistence.

A balance against bi-polar power politics, India emerged as an immense neutral nation. She is powerless in respect to nuclear weapons, but refuses to believe in the inevitability of war. India's statesmen have worked patiently toward the easing of world tensions and the reduction of world armament in the best interests of the United Nations—to save succeeding generations from the scourge of war. India has firmly opposed any acts of aggression or imperialism.

The political principles India has espoused reflect in so many ways the attitude of Gandhi; the official motto of the Republic of India states *Satyan Eva Jayate*—Truth Alone Prevails. Gandhi's life was a stepping-stone to the creation of truth in the world.

Much of India is still backward. She is trying to control her frightening birth rate, eliminate poverty, and industrialize on a large scale. She has diversified her economy and now trades freely with the other countries in the world, whereas at one time she could trade only with England.

Trade relations between the United States and India are particularly good. Many Indian firms have hired American engineers and technicians to help organize and develop new industry. Many Indians are furthering their education at American universities, as well as at other schools in the world.

Perhaps India may yet reflect the prayer and vision of Tagore, who wrote the lines quoted on page 88.

Bibliography

ALEXANDER, H. G. *The Indian Ferment*. London: Williams and Norgate, 1929.

————. *India Since Cripps*. London: Penguin Books, 1944.

ALL INDIA CONGRESS COMMITTEE. *Satyagraha in Gandhi's Own Words*. Allahabad, India, 1935.

AMBEDKAR, B. R. *Ranade, Gandhi and Jinnah*. Bombay: Thacker & Co., Ltd., 1943.

————. *What Congress and Gandhi Have Done to the Untouchables*. Bombay: Thacker & Co., Ltd., 1945.

ANDREWS, C. F. *Mahatma Gandhi's Ideas*. London: Allen & Unwin, 1929.

————. *Mahatma Gandhi: His Own Story*. New York: The Macmillan Company, 1931.

————. *Mahatma Gandhi At Work*. London: Allen & Unwin, 1931.

BERNAYS, ROBERT. *Naked Fakir*. London: Victor Gollancz, 1931.

BESANT, ANNIE. *How India Wrought For Freedom*. London: Theosophical Publishing House, 1915.

BEVAN, EDWYN. *Indian Nationalism*. New York: The Macmillan Company, 1914.

BOLITHO, HECTOR. *Jinnah*. London: John Murray, 1954.

BOSE, NIRMAL KUMAR. *Studies in Gandhism*. Calcutta: Indian Associated Publishing Company, 1947.

————. *Selections from Gandhi*. Ahmedabad, India: Navajivan Publishing House, 1948.

————. *My Days With Gandhi*. Calcutta: Nishana, 1953.

BOSE, SUBHAS CHANDRA. *The Indian Struggle*. London: Wishart, 1935.

CAMPBELL-JOHNSON, ALAN. *Mission With Mountbatten*. London: Robert Hale, 1951.

————. *Viscount Halifax*. London: Robert Hale, 1941.

CATLIN, GEORGE. *In the Path of Mahatma Gandhi*. London: Macdonald & Co., 1948.

CHAKRAVARTY, AMIYA. *Mahatma Gandhi and the Modern World*. Calcutta: Book House, 1945.

————(ed.). *A Tagore Reader*. Boston: Beacon Press, 1961.

CHINTAMANI, C. Y. *Indian Politics Since the Mutiny*. London: Allen & Unwin, 1939.

CHURCHILL, WINSTON. *The Second World War*. Vols. I, II, and IV. London: Cassell & Co., Ltd., 1948, 1950, and 1951.

COUPLAND, R. *The Constitutional Problem in India: A Restatement*. London: Oxford University Press, 1944.

CUMMING, SIR JOHN (ed.). *Political India, 1832-1932*. New York: Oxford University Press, 1932.

DANTWALALA, M. L. *Gandhism Reconsidered*. Bombay: Padma Publications, 1944.

DAS, BHAGAVAN. *The Science of the Self*. Benares, India: Indian Bookshop, 1939.

DATTA, DHIRENDRA M. *The Philosophy of Mahatma Gandhi*. Madison, Wisconsin: University of Wisconsin Press, 1961.

DESAI, MAHADEV. *Gandhi In Indian Villages*. Madras, India: S. Ganesan, 1928.

————. *With Gandhi in Ceylon*. Madras: S. Ganesan, 1928.

————. *The Story of Bardoli*. Ahmedabad: Navajivan Publishing House, 1929.

————. *Nation's Voice*. Ahmedabad: Navajivan Publishing House, 1932.

————. *The Epic of Tranvancore*. Ahmedabad: Navajivan Publishing House, 1937.

————. *Maulana Abul Kalam Azad*. London: Allen & Unwin, 1941.

————. *The Gita According to Gandhi*. Ahmedabad: Navajivan Publishing House, 1946.

————. *A Righteous Struggle*. Ahmedabad: Navajivan Publishing House, 1951.

————. *The Diaries*. Ahmedabad: Navajivan Publishing House, 1953.

DESHPANDE, P. G. *Gandhiana*. Ahmedabad: Navajivan Publishing House, 1948.

DHAWAN, G. N. *The Political Philosophy of Mahatma Gandhi*. Ahmedabad: Navajivan Publishing House, 1951.

DIWAKAR, R. R. *Satyagraha—Its Technique and History*. Bombay: Hind Kitabs, 1946.

————. *Glimpses of Gandhi*. Bombay: Hind Kitabs, 1949.

DOKE, JOSEPH J. *M. K. Gandhi*. Madras: G. A. Natesan & Co., 1909.

DUNCAN, RONALD (ed.). *Selected Writings of Mahatma Gandhi*. London: Faber & Faber, 1951.

EATON, JEANETTE. *Gandhi, Fighter Without a Sword*. New York: William Morrow & Co., 1950.

ELIOT, SIR CHARLES. *Hinduism and Buddhism: An Historical Sketch*. (3 vols.) New York: Longmans, Green & Company, 1921.

ELWIN, V. and J. WINSLOW. *The Dawn of Indian Freedom*. London: Allen & Unwin, 1931.

FISCHER, LOUIS. *The Life of Mahatma Gandhi*. New York: Harper & Brothers, 1950.

GANDHI, MOHANDAS K. *A Guide To Health*. Madras: S. Ganesan, 1921.

————. *Basic Education*. Ahmedabad: Navajivan Publishing House.

————. *Bapu's Letters to Mira (1924-1948)*. Ahmedabad: Navajivan Publishing House, 1949.

————. *Christian Missions*. Ahmedabad: Navajivan Publishing House, 1948.

————. *Constructive Programme*. Ahmedabad: Navajivan Publishing House, 1948.

————. *Community Unity*. Ahmedabad: Navajivan Publishing House, 1949.

————. *Delhi Diary*. Ahmedabad: Navajivan Publishing House, 1948.

————. *Diet and Diet Reform*. Ahmedabad: Navajivan Publishing House, 1949.

————. *Economics of Khadi*. Ahmedabad: Navajivan Publishing House, 1941.

————. *Ethical Religion*. Madras: S. Ganesan, 1922.

————. *For Pacifists*. Ahmedabad: Navajivan Publishing House, 1949.

————. *From Yiravda Mandir*. Ahmedabad: Navajivan Publishing House, 1937.

————. *Harijan* (newspaper). Ahmedabad: 1933-40, 1942, 1946-48.

————. *Gandhi's Correspondence With the Government (1942-44)*. Ahmedabad: Navajivan Publishing House, 1945.

————. *Hind Swaraj, or Indian Home Rule*. Ahmedabad: Navajivan Publishing House, 1938.

————. *Indian Opinion* (newspaper). Natal: 1904-14.

————. *Jail Experiences*. Madras: Tagore & Company, 1922.

————. *My Early Life*. Bombay: Oxford University Press, 1932.

————. *My Soul's Agony*. Ahmedabad: Navajivan Publishing House, 1932.

————. *Non-violence in Peace and War*. Ahmedabad: Navajivan Publishing House, (part I) 1945, (part II) 1949.

————. *Rebuilding Our Villages*. Ahmedabad: Navajivan Publishing House, 1952.

————. *Rowlatt Bills and Satyagraha*. Madras: G. A. Natesan & Co., 1919.

————. *Sarvodaya*. Ahmedabad: Navajivan Publishing House, 1951.

————. *Satyagraha*. Ahmedabad: Navajivan Publishing House, 1951.

————. *Satyagraha in South Africa*. Madras: S. Ganesan, 1928.

————. *Satyagraha Ashram's History*. Madras: G. A. Natesan & Co., 1933.

————. *Self-restraint v. Self-indulgence*. Ahmedabad: Navajivan Publishing House, 1947.

————. *Songs From Prison*. (adapted by John S. Hoyland) London: Allen & Unwin, 1934.

————. *Speeches and Writings*. Madras: G. A. Natesan & Co., 1933.

————. *The Story of My Experiments With Truth*. Washington, D.C.: Public Affairs Press, 1960.

————. *Towards New Education*. Ahmedabad: Navajivan Publishing House, 1953.

————. *Towards Non-violent Socialism*. Ahmedabad: Navajivan Publishing House, 1951.

————. *To Ashram Sisters*. Ahmedabad: Navajivan Publishing House, 1952.

————. *To a Gandhian Capitalist*. Bombay: Hind Kitabs, 1951.

————. *To the Students*. Ahmedabad: Navajivan Publishing House, 1949.

————. *Unto This Last*. Ahmedabad: Navajivan Publishing House, 1951.

————. *Women and Social Injustice*. Ahmedabad: Navajivan Publishing House, 1942.

————. *Young India* (newspaper). Ahmedabad: 1919-32.

GEORGE, S. K. *Gandhi's Challenge to Christianity*. London: Allen & Unwin, 1939.

GOVERNMENT OF INDIA. *Congress Responsibility for the Disturbances (1942-43)*. New Delhi, 1943.

————. *Gandhian Outlook and Techniques*. New Delhi, 1953.

————. *Homage to Gandhi*. New Delhi, 1948.

GREGG, RICHARD B. *A Discipline for Non-violence*. Ahmedabad: Navajivan Publishing House, 1941.

————. *The Power of Non-violence*. Ahmedabad: Navajivan Publishing House, 1938.

————. *Which Way Lies Hope?* Ahmedabad: Navajivan Publishing House, 1952.

HEATH, CARL. *Gandhi*. London: Allen & Unwin, 1944.

HINGORANI, A. T. *To the Students*. Karachi, Pakistan: The Author, 1935.

————. *To the Hindus and the Muslims*. Karachi, Pakistan: The Author, 1942.

————. *To the Princes and Their People*. Karachi, Pakistan: The Author, 1942.

————. *To the Protagonists of Pakistan*. Karachi, Pakistan: The Author, 1947.

HOLMES, JOHN HAYNES. *The Christ of Today*. Madras: Tagore & Company, 1922.

————. *My Gandhi*. New York: Harper & Brothers, 1953.

HOYLAND, JOHN S. *Indian Crisis*. New York: The Macmillan Company, 1944.

————. *The Cross Moves East*. London: Allen & Unwin, 1931.

JONES, M. E. *Gandhi Lives*. London: Hodder & Stoughton, 1948.

KALIKAR, KAKAR. *Stray Glimpses of the Bapu*. Ahmedabad: Navajivan Publishing House, 1950.

KIRPALANI, K. R. *Tagore, Gandhi and Nehru*. Bombay: Hind Kitabs, 1947.

LAJPAT, RAI LALA. *Ideals of Non-co-operation*. Madras: S. Ganesan, 1924.

————. *Unhappy India*. Calcutta: Banna Publishing Co., 1928.

LESTER, MURIEL. *Entertaining Gandhi*. London: Ivor Nicholson & Watson, 1932.

MAJUMDAR, R. C., *et al*. *An Advanced History of India*. New York: The Macmillan Company, 1946.

MASANI, R. P. *Dadabhai Naoroji*. London: Allen & Unwin, 1939.

MASHRUWALA, K. G. *Gandhi and Marx*. Ahmedabad: Navajivan Publishing House, 1951.

MEHTA, ASOKA and ACHYUT PATWARDHAN. *The Communal Triangle in India*. Allahabad: Kitabistan, 1942.

MIRABEHN. *Gleanings*. Ahmedabad: Navajivan Publishing House, 1949.

————. *Bapu's Letters to Mira*. Ahmedabad: Navajivan Publishing House, 1949.

MONTAGU, EDWIN S. *An Indian Diary*. London: William Heinemann, 1930.

MOULAND, W. H. and ATUL CHATTERJEE. *A Short History of India*. New York: Longmans, Green & Company, 1936.

MUKERJEE, HIRENDRANATH. *Indian Struggle for Freedom*. Bombay: Kutub, 1946.

MUZUMDAR, H. T. *Gandhi Triumphant! The Inside Story of the Historic Fast*. New York: Universal Publishing Co., 1939.

NAG, KALIDAS. *Tolstoy and Gandhi.* Patna, India: Pustak Bhandar, 1950.

NAIR, C. SANKARAN. *Gandhi and Anarchy.* Madras: Tagore and Company, 1922.

NANDA, B. R. *Mahatma Gandhi: A Biography.* Boston: Beacon Press, 1958.

NAYYAR, SUSHILA. *Kasturba.* Wellingford, Pennsylvania: Pendle Hill, 1948.

NEHRU, JAWAHARLAL. *An Autobiography.* London: John Lane, 1936.

————. *The Discovery of India.* Calcutta: Signet Press, 1941.

————. *Eighteen Months in India.* Allahabad: Kitabistan, 1938.

————. *Mahatma Gandhi.* Calcutta: Signet Press, 1949.

————. *The Unity of India.* London: Lindsay Drummond, 1941.

PATEL, G. I. *Life and Times of Vithalbhai.* Bombay: Books I & II, 1950.

PATEL, MANIBEHN. *Letters to Sardar Patel.* Ahmedabad: Navajivan Publishing House, 1950.

PRABHU, R. K. and U. R. RAO (ed.). *India of My Dreams.* Bombay: Hind Kitabs, 1947.

————. *The Mind of Mahatma Gandhi.* Bombay: Oxford University Press, 1945.

————. *Mahatma Gandhi and Bihar.* Bombay: Hind Kitabs, 1949.

PRASAD, RAJENDRA. *Gandhiji in Champaran.* Madras: S. Ganesan, 1928.

————. *India Divided.* Bombay: Hind Kitabs, 1947.

————. *Autobiography.* Muzaffarpur: Bharti Sadan, 1947.

————. *Satyagraha in Champaran.* Ahmedabad: Navajivan Publishing House, 1949.

PYARELAL. *The Epic Fast.* Ahmedabad: Navajivan Publishing House, 1932.

————. *A Pilgrimage For Peace.* Ahmedabad: Navajivan Publishing House, 1950.

————. *A Nation Builder At Work.* Ahmedabad: Navajivan Publishing House, 1953.

————. *Gandhian Techniques in the Modern World.* Ahmedabad: Navajivan Publishing House, 1953.

————. *Mahatma Gandhi, The Last Phase.* (2 vols.) Ahmedabad: Navajivan Publishing House, 1956 and 1957.

RADHAKRISHNAN, S. (ed.). *Mahatma Gandhi: Essays and Reflections.* London: Allen & Unwin, 1939.

————. *Indian Philosophy.* (2 vols.) London: Allen & Unwin, 1931.

RAJAGOPALACHARI, C. *The Nation's Voice.* Ahmedabad: Navajivan Publishing House, 1932.

RAMACHANDRAN, G. *A Sheaf of Gandhi Anecdotes.* Bombay: Hind Kitabs, 1946.

RAMAN, T. A. *What Does Gandhi Want?* New York: Oxford University Press, 1942.

RAO, R. V. *Gandhian Institutions of Wardha.* Bombay: Thackus, 1947.

RAVOOF, A. A. *Meet Mr. Jinnah.* Lahore: Sheikh Muhammad Ashraf, 1947.

ROLLAND, ROMAIN. *Mahatma Gandhi.* London: Allen & Unwin, 1924.

SEN, GERTRUDE EMERSON. *Voiceless India.* Toronto: Longmans, Green & Company, 1946.

SHAHANI, RANJU. *Mr. Gandhi.* New York: The Macmillan Company, 1961.

SHEEAN, VINCENT. *Lead Kindly Light.* New York: Random House, 1949.

————. *Mahatma Gandhi.* New York: Alfred A. Knopf, 1955.

SHRIDHARANI, KRISHNALAL. *War Without Violence.* New York: Harcourt Brace & Co., 1939.

————. *The Mahatma and the World.* New York: John Day Co., 1939.

SHUKLA, CHANDRASHANKAR (ed.). *Incidents of Gandhiji's Life.* Bombay: Vora & Co., 1949.

SINGH, ANUP. *Nehru, The Rising Star of India.* New York: John Day Co., 1939.

SITARAMAYZA, PATTABHI. *History of the Indian National Congress.* Vols. I and II. Bombay: Padma Publications, 1947.

SMITH, VINCENT. *The Oxford Student's History of India.* New York: Oxford University Press, 1951.

SMITH, WILFRED CANTWELL. *Modern Islam in India.* London: Victor Gollancz, 1947.

TAGORE, RABINDRANATH. *Mahatmaji and the Depressed Humanity.* Calcutta: Vishna-Bharati, 1932.

————. *Sadhana.* New York: The Macmillan Company, 1916.

TEMPLEWOOD, LORD. *Nine Troubled Years.* London: Collins, 1954.

TENDULKAR, D. G. *Mahatma.* (8 vols.) Bombay: Times of India Press, 1951-1954.

TENDULKAR, D. G., *et al.* (ed.). *Gandhiji: His Life and Work.* Bombay: Karnatak Publishing House, 1944.

TOYNBEE, ARNOLD. *The World and the West.* New York and London: Oxford University Press, 1953.

TUKER, FRANCIS. *While Memory Serves.* London: Cassell & Co., 1950.

UNITED NATIONS EDUCATIONAL, SCIENTIFIC, AND CULTURAL ORGANIZATION. *All Men Are Brothers: Life and Thoughts of Mahatma Gandhi.* Paris: UNESCO, 1958.

Vishna-Bharati Quarterly. "Gandhi, Memorial Peace Number." Santiniketan, 1949.

WALKER, ROY. *Sword of Gold.* London: Indian Independence Union, 1945.

————. *The Wisdom of Gandhi.* London: Andrew Pakers, Ltd., 1943.

WALLBANK, T. WALTER. *A Short History of India and Pakistan.* New York: Mentor, 1958.

WOOLACOTT, J. E. *India on Trial: A Study of Present Conditions.* New York: The Macmillan Company, 1929.

Index

Acknowledgments: Photographs on pages 2-3, 8, 20, 24, 68, 71, 77, 87, and 89 from the files of Wide World Photos, Inc.; photographs on pages 22, 36, and 40 from the files of the Information Service of India; photographs on pages 54 and 84 from the files of Brown Brothers; the photograph on page 31 from the files of Historical Pictures Service, and the photograph on page 63 from the files of the Radio Times Hulton Picture Library. Illustrations on pages 10-11, 12, 14, 16-17, 19, 26-27, 29, 32-33, 34, 42-43, 45, 46, 49, 51, 52, 60-61, 65, 66-67, 72, 74, 77, 79, 80, and 82-83 by Harley Shelton and Ron Kangles, Hollis Associates.